"The problem with training is that when the learners get back to work, people are waiting for them! Soon they're too busy to apply what they just learned, and the training investment is wasted. By implementing the expert strategies in this highly readable book, you can assure that the knowledge and skills people have learned are put into practice—and make the most of your training dollars."

—Ken Blanchard, co-author of *The New One Minute Manager* and *Servant Leadership in Action*

"DDI's Global Leadership Forecast reveals that over 50 percent of the highest quality leadership development occurs on the job—after the classroom concludes. However, executing this type of follow-up to formal learning can be incredibly challenging. The 7 Principles presented by the authors will help you powerfully reinforce learning and drive your talent and organizational strategies forward."

—Tacy M. Byham, Ph.D., CEO, DDI, and co-author of *Your First Leadership Job*

"As former CLO at Hilton, I know that reinforcement is needed to transfer learning into applying. The methodology of The 7 Principles of Reinforcement presented by the authors will help you to design an effective reinforcement program that creates lasting behavior change and an impact on your organization.

Thanks to the engaging stories, sports examples, and useful tools, this is one of the most readable books on reinforcement I've read."

—Kimo Kippen, VP, Global Workforce Initiatives, former Chief Learning Officer, Hilton

"I'm a believer. For the past few years I have transformed from being a client, to a practitioner, and ultimately to an evangelist of the reinforcement principles in this book. I've personally researched most of the alternative players in this industry, and while they are good at reminding and regurgitating, they don't get reinforcement like the authors do. If you want lasting change, employee and customer satisfaction, and revenue growth, then read and apply the principles in this book."

—Treion Muller, Chief Product Officer, TwentyEighty

"We all know the problem with corporate training. After the training the learner gets back to their work, they forget what they've been taught, and/or they're too busy to apply what they just learned. Nothing changes. The training investment is wasted.

A reinforcement program based on the methodology presented by the authors in The 7 Principles of Reinforcement solves this industry problem. I am convinced that this book helps you to create lasting behavior change and create impact in every organization.

It is your guarantee to increase productivity, improve communication, and boost the bottom line."

—Anne Stawiski, Global Business Owner, Learning Solutions, Amway

"I've been in many industries as a learning professional, from health care, to truck rental, food processing, and now the payments industry. Adult learning comes in a variety of delivery vehicles: e-learning, webinars, classroom, how-to videos, etc. The key is retention and how to get the intended audience to retain the knowledge gained from their learning experience. I believe The 7 Principles discussed in this book are a home run in terms of applying key reinforcement principles to help learners retain critical knowledge they have learned! By incorporating The 7 Principles of Reinforcement, I know that my intended audience will put what they have learned into practice, and to me, that is success!"

—Brian Condie, Director, Instructional Design, Visa Inc.

TRAINING REINFORCEMENT

TRAINING REINFORCEMENT

The 7 Principles to Create Measurable Behavior Change and Make Learning Stick

ANTHONIE WURTH

KEES WURTH

WILEY

For general information on our other products and services or for technical support, please contact our Customer Care Department within the United States at (800) 762–2974, outside the United States at (317) 572–3993 or fax (317) 572–4002.

Wiley publishes in a variety of print and electronic formats and by print-on-demand. Some material included with standard print versions of this book may not be included in e-books or in print-on-demand. If this book refers to media such as a CD or DVD that is not included in the version you purchased, you may download this material at http://booksupport.wiley.com. For more information about Wiley products, visit www.wiley.com.

Library of Congress Cataloging-in-Publication Data

Names: Wurth, Anthonie, 1967- author. | Wurth, Kees, 1969- author.
Title: Training reinforcement : The 7 Principles to create measurable
  behavior change and make learning stick / Anthonie Wurth, Kees Wurth.
Description: First Edition. | Hoboken : Wiley, 2018. | Includes
  bibliographical references and index. |
Identifiers:LCCN2018018080(print)|ISBN9781119425557(hardback)
Subjects: LCSH: Employees—Training of. | Employee motivation. | BISAC:
  BUSINESS & ECONOMICS / Training.
Classification:LCCHF5549.5.T7W872018(print   )
LC record available at https://lccn.loc.gov/2018018080

Printed in the United States of America

V080724_080418

This book is dedicated to people who changed my lasting behavior.
These special people influenced my life forever:

My parents, who did not change my life or behavior;
they helped me discover it.

My coach, Mr. Henneveld,
who developed my top sport mentality.

My wife, Monique, who continuously challenges me in
developing as a human being.

My three kids, Max, Sem, and Fleur, who changed the reason
why I am on earth.

My brother, Kees, whose behavior I admire and use as a
mirror to develop mine.

CONTENTS

INTRODUCTION

Corporations spend billions of dollars every year on employee training. These investments are meant to increase productivity, improve communication, and boost the bottom line, but often managers and executives feel as if they've thrown away their training dollars. Nothing changes.

The problem with corporate training is that when the learners get back to their work, they forget what they've been taught, and/or they're too busy to apply what they just learned. The training investment is wasted.

My brother, Kees, and I (Anthonie) wrote this book because we've seen this happen too many times. [Editor's note: Although Kees and Anthonie wrote this book together, "I" refers to Anthonie throughout the book.]

We are former top athletes who competed at the highest Judo level in the world. We spent many hours every day for many years becoming the best in our sport. We know how to train, and we know how to make training principles stick.

After my Judo career with experience as an Olympic athlete in 1992 in Barcelona, I was a corporate business trainer for knowledge and soft skills for more than ten years. When I compared how training was applied in the sports world versus the corporate world, I noticed a big difference. Training was given, but it was never followed up with reinforcement.

The combination of training and reinforcement is what transformed Kees and me from kids who liked to be physical into Judo champions. Without training reinforcement from our coach, we would never have made it to that level.

Solutions offered in the learning industry are good at regurgitating lessons and reminding learners of what they've been taught, but they don't reinforce lessons, which is required to create lasting behavior.

In this book, we describe an effective methodology that has proven its success in the last 12 years. We want to educate the learning industry and inspire every learning professional to see that reinforcement is much more than just sending reminders or a focus on knowledge retention.

By using this book, learning professionals can create a solid reinforcement program. The methodology used in *The 7 Principles of Reinforcement* is perfectly balanced between engagement and results. Using The 7 Principles we describe, you can develop a program that reinforces learning and drives your talent and organizational strategies forward. Then you can be assured that the knowledge and skills your learners have been trained in are put into practice and that you are spending your training dollars well.

By applying The 7 Principles of Reinforcement, you drive training results and increase learners' engagement. A strong reinforcement program with a focus on results, but with no participation, does not create lasting behavior change or impact in your organization. But high engagement does not always guarantee good outcomes. Only the perfect balance between a strong foundation with measurable results and a focus on engagement guarantees the transfer of training from learning into application.

We have divided the book into four parts, and throughout the book we use a lot of examples from our sports careers to explain The 7 Principles and the methodology.

Part 1 explains how you can achieve behavior change by using reinforcement. We explain what reinforcement is, what is needed for behavior change, the difference between training goals and reinforcement objectives, and what influences behavior change.

In Part 2, we provide an overview of The 7 Principles of Reinforcement, and then explain how the first three principles are used to build a strong foundation to drive results. Chapters 6, 7, and 8 contain tools and assessments to help you to build and improve your foundation.

Part 3 helps you build your engagement to increase learners' participation. In Chapters 10, 11, and 12 we explain the three principles that help you create messages that will reinforce the training and keep your learners' minds engaged. Again, each chapter provides tools and assessments.

To analyze your reinforcement program, you will find a more detailed look at the methodology in Part 4. A methodology based on your specific reinforcement lever helps you determine when improvement is needed. Chapter 16 suggests ways to check and improve your reinforcement messages. The S.A.F.E. methodology is based on 12 years of analyzing reinforcement messages and determining their impact.

Chapter 17 explains the different approaches by training type. Chapter 18 provides you the best practices on how to introduce training reinforcement programs in your organization and explains the role facilitators have in a successful reinforcement program. In Chapter 19 we describe the final recommodations to become a reinforcement expert.

The Appendix contains all the tools you need to build an effective reinforcement program. Also make sure to visit www.the7principlesofreinforcement.com, where you will find digital versions of all the assessments, tests, and action plans, along with reporting options. You can also download additional reinforcement programs based on this book.

WE DID IT!

Winning an Olympic gold medal is not easy. I never won one; neither did my brother, Kees.

Writing a book is also not easy. But we did it! I am so proud of our accomplishment. It feels like our gold medal. You never win gold alone. I want to thank many people.

My wife, Monique, who listened for two years to all the ideas I had. My son Max (20 years old) who was part of the research team, my son Sem (14 years old) who asked lots of questions while he practiced his English via this book, and my daughter Fleur (12) who assisted me with food and drinks while I was writing.

Besides all the other people who read the book, gave feedback, and asked lots of questions to help me improve this book, I want to thank my late coach, Koos Henneveld, who asked me the "two questions." My parents, Wout Wurth and Nennie van der Matten, who always showed their pride during our journey of writing this book.

Finally, I want to thank my soul mate, brother, business partner, and co-author Kees for all his input and support and for being a sparring partner not only on the Judo mat but also on paper. This time we did it!

PART 1

UNDERSTANDING REINFORCEMENT TO REACH BEHAVIOR CHANGE

You train your employees until you think you can't teach them anything else, but you aren't seeing the results you expect or want. What's the problem? Where's the disconnect?

You're missing the reinforcement component: the application of what people have learned. Reinforcement is required to change behavior and to reach the outcomes you seek.

The chapters in this part of the book explain what reinforcement is, how behavior change happens, and how you can influence behavior change in your learners.

CHAPTER 1

Eyeing Gold

"Clean up your sports bags." This is what my mum and dad said every day when my brother and I came home from our Judo training. For some reason, we were in the habit of dropping our sports bags right behind the door when we entered the house.

Kees, my younger brother, and I trained in the Dutch national selection for Judo. Our sports bags contained Judo suits, wet towels, our Judo belts, and materials to prevent injuries. Those bags were heavy—probably too heavy to carry them inside to the scullery where the washing machine was. As soon as we put one foot in the house, we dropped the bags. (Maybe this bad habit runs in the family, because I recognize the same behavior with my kids, and so does Kees.)

My dad had his own company and always came home late. As soon as he opened the door, he needed to "climb" inside. In a loud, irritated voice, he let us know that our behavior was not acceptable. But for some reason, we could not change this behavior. I must admit, perhaps we did not try hard enough and we were just lazy.

If I remember correctly, this laziness was the only behavior that didn't suit our role as top athletes in martial arts. Judo is a Japanese martial art that requires a lot of discipline and respect. It also requires lots of practice to master all the skills.

LAYING THE GROUNDWORK

Kees and I began taking Judo lessons when we were five years old. We attended classes at a local sports club with lots of other kids. Mum and dad spent lots of hours driving us to the club and then waiting to drive us home, just as lots of other parents do.

When I was 12, we started riding our bikes to the club. Using bikes is a common means of transport in Holland. When we came home after a two-hour

3

training session, we would park our bikes in the garage and drop our sports bags on the floor. We trained seven days a week, and every day my father saw our bags behind the door. "Clean up your bags!" he'd shout. For some reason, we could not change this behavior.

In our teenage years, Kees and I were part of Holland's national team. We traveled a lot and won medals at international tournaments. Judo became our life. All of our teachers at school knew that we could not always be present in class or had to leave early for training.

Our friends knew we would not join them when there was a party or a birthday with cake. Judo athletes compete in different weight classes, so at every tournament, the athletes must weigh in to check their body weight for the class they will compete in. Kees and I fought in different weight classes. My mother was happy that we never had an official fight against each other.

When we weren't training, we were thinking about food. Kees and I both had to lose a lot of weight before each competition. Our fat percentage was extremely low, and we could not eat a lot the week before the weigh-in. Our diets consisted of well-balanced meals. Sweets and candy were rare treats. The benefit of living on a strict diet was that our family and friends accepted our behavior and did not offer any drinks, candies, cake, or food that was not good for a top athlete. With so few temptations, it was quite easy to stick to a strict diet.

The same for our rest. We slept, rested, and prepared ourselves for the next training. We did this 365 days a year for many years. Our life was different from most young men's. We did not drink, and we did not go to parties, birthday celebrations, or summer camps. We lived in locker rooms, sports halls, and airports—and on the Judo mat. Without being aware of what we were doing, we slowly changed our lives and our behavior. Except for the sports bags.

In 1987, I had finished my Judo training for the day; I was in the locker room. I was tired and sitting on a wooden bench. My coach Koos Henneveld entered the room, and I looked up.

"Anthonie, do you want to become an Olympic champion?" he asked.

"Yes."

My coach stepped closer and looked into my eyes and asked a second question. "Anthonie, is it also your choice?"

"Yes," I said again, not exactly knowing what this would mean for the rest of my sports career.

For the next five years, I followed a strict diet; my schooling was extended by two years, and I had a girlfriend but hardly saw her. I lived for a year in Japan. I trained more than 20 hours a week. My strength, my flexibility, my conditioning—everything—was measured.

We went to tournaments, completed evaluations to determine our improvement, did repetitions of specific moves more than 2,000 times a day. My whole life was a consequence of my choice.

In 1991, I won several international medals and became the European champion at a tournament in Prague. Based on these results, I was selected for the Dutch Olympic Team to represent the Netherlands in the Barcelona 1992 Olympics.

My coach also coached Kees, who is two years younger than I am and a talented athlete. Five years before the Olympic games in 1992, my coach asked him the same two questions: "Do you want to become an Olympic champion?" and "Is it your choice?" Kees also answered yes to both questions.

Kees also did all the hard work, trained 20 hours a day, followed a strict diet, and lived the life of a top athlete. When it was time for him to go to Japan, the Mecca of the Judo sports, for more training, he chose to go to the United States instead through an exchange program at his school.

He lived in the United States for almost seven months. During that time, the hard daily training, the diet, and the life of a top athlete became less of a priority. When he returned to Holland in 1990, he realized that he had only answered yes to the first question, "Do you want to become an Olympic champion?" Answering the second question yes and facing all the consequences of your choice is extremely difficult.

Kees was inspired by me and started to train again when he returned. He trained extremely hard, as if he were punishing himself for the seven months of not living like a top athlete. When I looked at his training effort, I felt I need to do more, too. That year, 1990, was our best training year ever.

In 1991 Kees became Dutch champion and won many medals at international tournaments, but it was not enough to qualify him for the Dutch Olympic Team. Competing at the top level of a sport is hard, very hard. Kees realized that the results he achieved were not enough and were a consequence of his choices. "That is how it works," Kees said when we heard he was not selected for the Dutch Olympic Team.

Kees became my sparring partner for the last part of "our" Olympic journey. He trained with me every day. He ate the same food as I did. He was always there when I needed him.

HEADED TO THE OLYMPICS

It was 1992. The Olympic Judo tournament was conducted at the Palau Blau-grana Arena. After all those years of focus, the day—Thursday, July 30, 1992—was finally here. This day had been marked on our calendar for years.

Based on my results I was favored to win the gold medal. In the first part of the program, every fight was perfect; they all went just as planned. I didn't have any trouble with my opponents. Every hour we came closer to our gold medal.

At the end of the day, only a few athletes were left. They all won their fights, and these final rounds decided who became Olympic champion. I had to fight an American. After five minutes, I lost with a minimum score. I still feel pain from this memory. When I left the fighting arena, I was crying. I was a broken athlete. I lost my gold medal. I lost my dream. I lost!

A Japanese athlete whom I defeated in 1991 at the World Championships won the gold. That made my loss even more painful. With tears in our eyes, Kees and I listened to the Japanese anthem during the medal ceremony at the end of the day—silent, anonymous, somewhere at the top of the stands. We left the Palau Blaugrana Arena in silence.

We realized that our dream was finished. We couldn't live another four years under this extreme training regimen. Even if we did, we would not become better contenders for the gold medal than I was in 1992. Days after the competition, we evaluated our performance. Now I had two questions for my coach that had been running through my mind for the last few days:

"Why did I lose?"

"What did I do wrong?"

Sitting at the pier in the Olympic Village, my coach answered me:

"Anthonie, you did not do anything wrong."

"But why didn't I win the gold medal? What did I do wrong?"

He looked out over the sea before answering. "If you do not do anything, you cannot do it wrong! You should take initiatives. You should attack to win. Only waiting and defense is not the way to win gold." Then he paused. The silence created impact.

"You have to take initiative to win the gold medal," he repeated. He stood and helped me up. "It's the same in life. Mark that in your mind."

I was speechless. While I thought about what he had just said, he walked away. He held his head upright and stately. His job was done. He had also lost gold.

Although I didn't know it at the time, this is the fundamental principle of a successful reinforcement program: "Take initiative."

After our Judo careers ended, Kees and I continued our lives as entrepreneurs. Kees moved to the United States and created and built up his company. I stayed in Holland and joined the corporate training industry. Using the same high-level sports mentality we grew up with, we have both succeeded in growing our businesses. Every day someone is waiting for you to take initiative!

Kees runs a retail business. He knows that "retail is detail," exactly like top-level sports. You must pay close attention to the details. There is no shortcut to the gold medal. Kees has never lost his sports mentality.

I joined Europe's biggest training company. I have trained thousands of groups on soft skills, such as communication, leadership, sales, presentation skills, and cultural change, as well as holding many individual coaching sessions.

After 10 years in the training industry, I feel comfortable comparing corporate training to athletic training. What is the difference between the way Olympic athletes train and how employees in corporations train? Not many athletes can compare their lives as athletes with life in the corporate training world. Only long experience in both worlds allows them to understand both worlds and to compare the two.

OLYMPIC TRAINING VERSUS CORPORATE TRAINING

After spending more than 10 years training as a top-level athlete and working for 10 years as a corporate trainer and consultant, I started to compare the results of various sports training methods to corporate training.

In top-level sports, everybody knows the 10,000-hour rule. The key to achieving world-class expertise in your field is to practice in a correct way for a total of 10,000 hours. A quick calculation shows that 10,000 hours is three hours of training per day for 52 weeks per year for 10 years. I did not see that happening in the corporate world. In the 1990s, training consisted of a two-day classroom event and maybe a follow-up after a couple of months.

I also noticed that the results of training in the corporate world were rarely measured. At the end of training sessions, learners might give feedback on how the training was and how the trainer performed. But that's not what matters.

Training outcomes should focus on the effect of the training, how it influenced behavior change, its impact in the organization. In sports, everything is measured—your speed, your condition, your fat percentage, your strength, how you performed in the training, the competition. Everything is analyzed to determine the next training period. Everything is focused on the performance and getting results.

In the corporate training industry, everything seemed to be focused on the training itself: How well did the trainer do? Did HR select the correct training? Does it help you in your daily work life? Evaluation and reflection are valuable approaches in top-level sports. Every tournament, every performance gets a solid evaluation. Every athlete is realistic about receiving an honest evaluation.

When I became the Dutch Judo champion, my coach came to me and said, "Anthonie, tomorrow morning, 8 a.m." I replied that 8 a.m. was a bit early for a party. He told me, "Remember, our goal is not to become Dutch champion. Our goal is Olympic champion." So we evaluated the championship match and determined what details to work on next. We did this every day. Our evaluation always started with self-reflection. My team of coaches carefully listened to how I thought the tournament went and how I thought I could improve. We talked not only about the tournament but also about the food, the training, the preparations, the coaching, everything.

In corporate training, I see a lot of underutilized assessment tools. I am convinced that behavior change starts when you can perform a good self-reflection. If you cannot identify your own necessary improvements, you are probably not aware of them. Behavior change starts with Awareness.

Just after the millennium, I started to investigate how I could combine lessons learned from the top-level sport world and the corporate training world. What did I know from both worlds, and how could I implement some synergy?

I figured out that, strangely enough, a conflict of interest exists between the client and the trainer in the corporate world. The trainers' business model at that time was not based on results. They earned money by holding classroom training or training events. The more events, the more money. The client, in contrast, wanted to employ the training outcomes as long as possible. So the trainer earns money with more training events, but the clients want to profit from the training as long as possible. Imagine what would happen if this occurred in sports! In top-level sports, the athlete and the trainer or coach have the same goal—results at the highest level.

By asking: What is more important than the training itself? I could solve the conflict of interest. The answer is: The period after a training event. The most important part of training should be how people apply what they have learned in the training.

When I competed in Judo, the work with my coach wasn't important. It was all about the way I applied and used the Judo techniques he taught me. The important part wasn't how I trained or whether I remembered the moves or how often we trained. It was how I applied what I learned, how I changed my behavior, my Judo moves, when I had to perform.

The bridge between the training event and applying what you have learned is called *reinforcement*!

CHAPTER 2

What Is Reinforcement?

Companies often attempt to solve a business problem through classroom training or e-learning courses, but find it difficult to apply specific training goals and measure training results. I have these conversations every day.

New knowledge and skills start to fade as soon as your learners leave the training. In fact, 90 percent of learners quickly forget the new knowledge and skills learned in training and revert to old habits. It is as if the training never took place at all! This severely threatens the ultimate goal of increasing knowledge retention and driving lasting behavior change.

Can you imagine how that would work in an Olympic program?

While organizations invest a lot of time, money, and resources in their training programs, the training doesn't stick and the impact is very low. So how do you move learners into actively applying their new skills and knowledge back on the job? In this chapter, you will learn how the brain works, why your learners forget, and what is needed for behavior change.

THE EFFECT OF MIND-SET ON LEARNING

Before we discuss why your learners forget what they've learned and how to create behavior change, it's important to understand how the brain works. Our brains not only store all of the new information we learn, but they also retrieve information when we need it. How can you help your brain be more invested in learning and better trained in storage, stickiness, and retrieval?

If you understand why people attend training programs in the first place, the design of your reinforcement program will be much easier. You may think that people think about the benefits of learning and choose the best option for their future. That is usually not the case.

The Prospect Theory describes the way human beings make decisions. Instead of choosing the most beneficial situation that may exist, people place more value on what they could lose than on any benefits they may get from an unknown future. So when deciding to invest time to learn, grow, and change their behavior, the learners rate the potential losses higher than the potential benefits.

Consider this scenario. Would you choose option A or option B:

A. Receive $900.

B. Take a 90 percent chance of winning $1,000 (and a 10 percent chance of winning $0).

Did you avoid the risk and choose option A, the $900? Most people do, although the expected outcome is the same in both cases.

However, if I asked you to choose between the next options, which one would you choose?

A. Lose $900.

B. Take a 90 percent chance of losing $1,000.

You would probably prefer option B and thus engage in risk-seeking behavior in the hope of avoiding the loss.

Your learners also tend to overweigh options that are certain and to be risk-averse for gains. We would rather have an assured, lesser win than take the chance at winning more (but also risk possibly getting nothing). The opposite is true when dealing with certain losses: learners engage in risk-seeking behavior to avoid a certain loss.

When your learners need to change their behavior, they are not always assured of a win. The result of using what they've learned is an unknown for the learner: "Will I succeed?" If they change their behavior successfully, they probably "win" more, that is, they reach a higher performance level, have more impact, or receive a promotion. What if they don't succeed? In the learner's mind, practicing the new behavior you are trying to reinforce can be seen as a risk. On the other hand, if the company insists on behavioral change because it's needed to improve the company's performance, your learner will probably take the risk instead of losing his job.

If your learner participates in your follow-up reinforcement program, they always have to deal with unknowns and risk-seeking behavior. They are thus critical, and you continually need to add value—in your content, in your timing, in your communication, in your style of writing, in your use of media, in your approach to driving participation, in your complete program. Encourage learners to think of what they will learn and can achieve with your program.

If you add the learner's mind-set to the training decision, it becomes even more interesting. How does the learner think about their current skills and behavior? If they have a fixed mind-set, they have fixed ideas about their current skills; they don't have any interest in trying new things because the learning may expose that they are not smart enough or they don't know how to do something that the new skill is based on. If you look in your organization, you probably will recognize this mind-set. You may also recognize the people with a completely opposite mind-set, a growth mind-set. This type of learner likes to take on more challenges and try new things, even if they may fail or their primary focus is on something other than growth and improvement.

If you want to change behavior in an environment that contains learners with both mind-sets, focus your program on the growth mind-set and on the future benefits that will help your learners overcome the Prospect Theory. Unfortunately, those who choose to "win" and possess a growth mind-set are not obvious, which makes behavior change a challenge. The use of The 7 Principles of Reinforcement will help you a lot.

In top-level sports, the Prospect Theory and the right mind-set are important. My coach taught me that Judo, as a martial art, is a mind game. He always said, "It's not the other Judo player who can beat you, it's your brain that makes you lose." He started with some mind coaching when I was young. He started with "Believe in yourself," "Have trust in the time and effort you spent in the preparation." Later, in preparation for the Olympics, we spent a lot of time understanding how one's mind-set influences performance.

During a Judo tournament, opponents fight five or six times per day, and if you win a match, you move to the next round. If you lose, the competition for that day is over. No rematch, no medal, and no success. This is what top athletes hate the most.

In the beginning of my career, I lost countless fights in the last minute, not because of my condition but because of the way I thought. In the 1990s a Judo fight lasted five minutes. In most of my fights, I scored more points in the first four minutes than my opponent did. So, with one minute to go, I was the winner. During that last minute, my brain would start to work at maximum speed. "What if I lose?" "What if I can't stop his attacks?" "I can't keep this going for another minute." "What if. . . ."

All the thoughts were negative. They were focused on losing what I had—the good score and a winning position. My biggest opponent was myself. With thoughts of losing the winning position, my brain decided not to attack anymore, but to switch to defense. It was the Prospect Theory in action. Instead of continuing to attack, I would think of how I could "survive" my opponent's attacks. Because he was in exactly the opposite situation, he needed to attack to win the game. In his situation, he had nothing to lose, so his brain chose to attack and go for the win. It was classic Prospect Theory: engaging in risk-seeking behavior in the hope of avoiding a loss.

The winning Judo player is defensive near the end of the match, and the losing player is active. Because Judo is a refereed sport, the player who tries to defend himself receives penalties. When penalties are levied, points are awarded to the opponent. Even when an opponent fails to score a point with an attack, he gains points because of the penalties. Switching to a more defensive approach (the Prospect Theory) after I had been successful for four minutes by using an attack approach was not good. I learned over time not to switch; I had to believe in the win instead of avoiding the loss.

An old piece of Judo wisdom I heard when I lived in Japan expresses this mind game exactly: "Attack is the best defense." So even when your brain wants to avoid losing, don't change to a defensive approach; stay in the attack mode.

Over the years, I learned how to challenge my brain in a way that would support my decisions to attack and to grow. This mind game is happening all the time for everyone. You need to understand what is happening and avoid assuming that all learners automatically believe in the benefits of your program. As I mentioned before, always add value for the learner and encourage learners to think of what they will learn and can achieve with your program.

If you want to build a strong reinforcement program and make maximum use of the way our brains work, remember that the human brain likes contrast. Instead of learning XXXX YYYY, learn XYXYXYXY. In Chapter 11, you will learn all about the balance between direction and friction. The learners may feel confused, but they are learning better.

MEMORIES AND EMOTIONS PLAY A ROLE

For the retrieving part of learning retention, memories and emotions are important. In your brain, the hippocampus stores and produces memories, and your amygdala stores and produces emotions.

That combination of memories and emotions is a solid foundation for successful behavior change. Before you design your program, evaluate your current training. How intense are the learning memories and emotions that the learners create? Is your training more like a lecture, or is it experiential learning?

An Olympic athlete's training is all about memories and emotions. My body still reacts to a specific word that my coach used over and over again. No matter whether it was spoken during an intense training on the beach, a very technical training in the gym, an evaluation session, or a lecture, that word has been stored in my brain and connected with all kind of situations, smells, feelings, frustrations, and successes. It wasn't difficult to retrieve then and isn't difficult to retrieve today. That word still excites me, even though I finished my Judo career in 1993. Initiative!

If you use media or expressions in your reinforcement program, use the same images, sayings, words, or expressions you used in the training event. The hippocampus and amygdala work together to help your learners retrieve feelings and emotions about the topic. This combination makes the retrieval more intense and valuable for behavioral change.

YOU WILL FORGET

To encourage retrieval, the brain must be challenged at the appropriate time and at the point of forgetting. The 7 Principles I describe in this book will help you to determine the appropriate timing and challenges the brain needs to change behavior. Before you invest time and effort to master The 7 Principles of Reinforcement, let's take a closer look at the point of forgetting.

When are these forgetting points? Back in 1885, Hermann Ebbinghaus, a German psychologist, began an experimental study on the relative strength of memory over a short period of time. In his experiment, Ebbinghaus repeatedly tested subjects' retention of various nonsense syllables over a variety of time periods. From his studies, Ebbinghaus plotted what is now called the Forgetting Curve (see Figure 2.1).

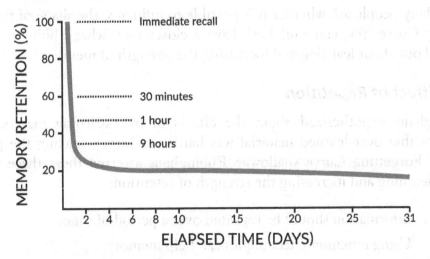

Figure 2.1. The Forgetting Curve

How Much Learning Is Forgotten?

If you take a close look at the Forgetting Curve, you will see that 70 percent of all training is forgotten after 24 hours. The curve decreases less steeply after two days and stays the same. The most material is lost in the first two days after the training event.

I try to find ways to improve learning retention. Over the last 12 years, I have asked many learners the same questions about forgetting. I explain that remembering what was presented in a training event is an important first step to being able to put what you learned into practice. Retaining information is fundamental to behavior change.

If I asked you to answer the following question, what would you say?

How much of what was presented during the last training event you attended can you recall?

1. I can remember most of what was presented (90 to 100 percent).
2. I can remember 75 to 90 percent of what was presented.
3. I can remember about 50 to 75 percent of what was presented.
4. I can remember about 20 to 50 percent of what was presented.
5. I can remember no more than 20 percent of what was presented.

It doesn't matter where I am when I ask this question. The answer that learners select most often is answer choice 5: "I remember no more than 20 percent of what was presented." [Of course, I receive different answers if I ask this question right after a training event.]

Many people ask whether it is possible to influence the shape of the Forgetting Curve. Yes, you can! Let's have a closer look what Ebbinghaus also figured out about learning and increasing the strength of memory.

The Effect of Repetition

Ebbinghaus hypothesized about the effects of over-learning material. He thought that over-learned material was harder to forget, making the participants' Forgetting Curve shallower. Ebbinghaus asserted these three things about learning and increasing the strength of retention:

1. Information should be repeated over a period of time.
2. Using mnemonic techniques can help memory.
3. The material that is presented should be meaningful.

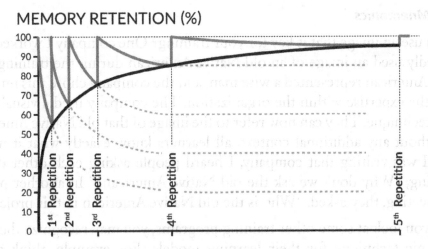

Figure 2.2. The Effect of Repetition on Forgetting

With each repetition of the material, your learners retain more information. The Forgetting Curve shows that learners forget the most material in the first 24 hours, so you should start as soon as your training event ends.

Figure 2.2 illustrates that a repetition moment interrupts the descending line of the Forgetting Curve. If you also look at the timing of the repetitions, you will notice that the Forgetting Curve is less steep after each repetition. This means that, over a period of time, you don't need as many repetitions as in the beginning.

If you think you only need five repetitions for your learners to remember the material and change their behavior, I must disappoint you. A reinforcement program is much more than increasing the strength of a memory. It's crucial to retrieve the learning, so let's focus next on the use of mnemonic techniques, which Ebbinghaus also mentioned.

Mnemonics Aid Recall

Mnemonics are proven to help learners recall information. There are many types of mnemonics, each of which is best suited to remembering different types of learning materials. Look at your training materials; undoubtedly you also use mnemonics. Many companies use mnemonics to make complex information more easily remembered. I have studied many training programs in the last 12 years, and I have found two categories used repeatedly:

- *Visual:* use of memorable images.
- *Verbal:* terms organized in a distinctive pattern.

Visual Mnemonics

Do you use an image that is key for your training? One company I worked with repeatedly used an image of an old Native American during the training. The Native American represented a wise man, and the company chose this image to reflect the expertise within the organization. The company used a visual mnemonic technique. They can now refer to the image of that old Native American, and without any additional context, all learners know exactly what it means. When I was visiting that company, I heard people asking each other during a meeting, "Why don't we ask the old Native American?" In another project team meeting, they asked, "Who is the old Native American in this project?"

If you look at some other training programs, you may recognize the same mnemonic technique for their learning models. For example, think of the model that Stephen R. Covey uses in his book *The 7 Habits of Highly Effective People* or Ken Blanchard for his Situational Leadership® II, or DDI uses for its Key Principles. After you complete this book and try the methods I offer, you will probably add a new image to your memory—an image of The 7 Principles of Reinforcement®.

Verbal Mnemonics

Verbal mnemonic techniques are often used in addition to visual mnemonics. When I help my kids with their learning, I always like to create a word so they remember the information, for example, "four important characteristics of a landscape" or "five steps of a formula."

As business people, we all know SWOT (strengths, weaknesses, opportunities, and threats) or SMART (specific, measurable, attainable, realistic, and timely), correct? I use the same mnemonic technique with my kids, and you can create verbal mnemonics for your training.

Meaningful Materials and Timing

Ebbinghaus also mentioned the use of "meaningful" materials for increasing the strength of the memory. Meaningful materials include:

- Key words from a learning session.
- An image that describes the essence of a model.
- Text without too much expository information.

In reinforcement programs, I see lots of ballast materials—handouts filled with general explanations. Designers of reinforcement programs seem to have trouble with "less is more." When you continue reading this book and learn The 7 Principles of Reinforcement, you will know how to select and write meaningful information. It's not as obvious as it seems; be prepared.

Meaningful also has to do with timing. If your learners are not aware of the importance of new information, the new information is not meaningful. Only the information that helps your learners understand *why* they have to learn or do something is meaningful in the Awareness phase. I explain more about meaningful information in Chapter 3.

CHAPTER 3

Behavior Change Is Critical

The Forgetting Curve illustrates the case that new knowledge must be continuously reinforced over a period of time, using mnemonic techniques and meaningful material. But focusing on knowledge isn't enough.

When I was training in Poland, my coach and I had countless coaching sessions in hotel rooms that never varied, no matter what hotel we were staying in. My coach always sat in the chair with his small black notebook, and I always sat on one of the beds. We would evaluate my performance after a training or tournament.

In the beginning of my career, we spent many hours on one specific question: "I know how to do it, so why did I not do it?"

My coach helped me to find out what was blocking me from doing what I knew how to do. He challenged me over and over again and slowly repeated, "You don't win medals by remembering how to do it, but by doing it when it's needed."

My frustrated reaction was either, "I know how to do it!" or "Of course I remember what I need to do!"

Eventually my coach would leave the room, and I would look at the ceiling, trying to find an answer and hearing his words: "You don't win medals by remembering how to do it, but by doing it when it's needed."

Knowing and remembering are not enough to achieve results, although learners must start by gaining knowledge and skills and being able to retrieve information. But they need to do more.

Since my coaching sessions in those small hotel rooms, I have been looking for answers and am convinced that there must be something more important than Ebbinghaus's Forgetting Curve. But what? The answer: If you want to overcome the Forgetting Curve, you must focus on behavioral change.

Without teaching behavioral change, you are merely reminding your learners of what they were taught. Achieving behavior change through your training program is the same as winning a gold medal. The focus must be on "doing it when it's needed." For example, you can train your learners on the importance of wearing a safety helmet while on a construction site. You can follow up on that training by sending reminders to them daily, weekly, or monthly. However, this does not mean they will wear their helmets. If you want all learners to wear their helmets, they must change their behavior. Knowing helmets are necessary is not enough.

PHASES OF BEHAVIOR CHANGE

Successful behavior change always requires 3 phases. No exceptions! Each phase has a specific role in a successful change. You cannot skip one or use a different order. Of course, each phase will vary in length and design, depending on the learner.

The phases are:

1. The Awareness phase.
2. The Knowledge/Skills phase.
3. The Apply phase.

If you want to change your learners' behavior, remember how the brain works. Based on the Prospect Theory (discussed in Chapter 2), you know that your learners place more value on any potential losses in their current situations than on any benefits they may get from the unknown future. So, a balanced, step-by-step process is needed to help your learners understand why and how they can change their behavior. If you mess up this process, you will not achieve behavior change and not win your "gold medal."

The Awareness Phase

During the Awareness phase, your learner starts to understand and accept *why* the change is needed. The brain will continue the thinking process only if your learner understands why the change is needed. If it's not clear, the brain will keep asking, "*Why* do I need to change?" It doesn't make any sense to continue training and expect a behavior change if learners' brains are focused on this question. If their brains understand and accept the why, they are ready for the next phase.

The Knowledge/Skills Phase

In the next phase, you will see that learners' brains focus on the question of how: "I understand *why* I have to change, but *how* do I do that?" This is the Knowledge and Skills phase.

During this phase, your learners will collect all of the new knowledge and skills needed for behavior change. They need to answer the "how" question with: "I know how to do it." That does not mean the behavior change is successful yet. Remember what my coach told me in the small hotel rooms: "You don't win medals by remembering *how* to do it, but by *doing* it when it's needed."

The Apply Phase

Only when learners' brains know why and how to change, can the Apply phase begin. During this phase, the learners' focus is on *doing* it. They want to know: "*What* do I need to *do*?" This is when the learners put the new behavior into practice.

The first Principle of Reinforcement is to Master the 3 Phases. If you do, you will begin to build an important part of your reinforcement foundation. I will explain in detail how to master all the phases later in the book.

MEANINGFUL INFORMATION

If you want to achieve behavior change, you must use meaningful materials. What is *meaningful* information for behavior change? Do you know?

When you design your reinforcement program and select meaningful information, consider the different characteristic of each phase. For example, in the Awareness phase, it's meaningful to use facts, figures, or graphs that help the learners understand why change is important. To check whether information is meaningful, consider whether the information helps answer the learners' questions, summarized in Table 3.1.

Table 3.1.   Selecting Meaningful Information

The Behavior Change Phases	The Learners' Questions
Awareness	*Why* do I have to change?
Knowledge/Skills	*How* do I have to change?
Apply	*What* do I need to *do*?

If you use only the Forgetting Curve as the basis of your reinforcement program, you won't achieve behavior change within your organization. According to Ebbinghaus, you should remind your learners of the material you want them to know five times before they retain the knowledge. Wouldn't it be amazing if your learners could remember everything you taught them after only five repetitions?

Unfortunately, in daily practice, five repetitions are not enough. Some research shows that meaningful material must be repeated at least 20 times before it sticks.

To master my Judo moves, a 10,000-hour rule was more realistic. Let's have a closer look at these 10,000 hours of training. Kees and I always trained very hard. We left little puddles of sweat wherever we performed our moves, and every time we left the gym or the dojo (Japanese for training room), we could barely walk. We enjoyed the feeling of working hard and the feeling that our efforts got us somewhere.

In the summer of 1989, I heard that the Russian team changed their approach and spent much more time in specific 14-day training camps. I told my coach I wanted to train more. In my mind, it was not an option to lose to the Russian guy just because he trained more. If they trained more, I would train more, too.

The coach started the conversation with some questions: "Anthonie, do you have a clear goal?"

"Yes, coach."

"Anthonie, is your training schedule clear, and do you have just enough direction?"

"Yes, coach"

"Anthonie, is your problem a lack of effort?"

"No, coach"

"Anthonie, do you know what creates results?"

"Yes, a clear goal, good training program, and hard work."

My coach looked at me and paused before he said, "It's not the intensity but the consistency that creates results."

He explained that you achieved fewer results if you went to a 14-day training camp and trained for eight hours per day instead of training two hours every week for a whole year.

My coach said, "Anthonie, winning gold and creating results is a marathon, not a sprint. All your effort and intensity are nothing without consistency." As he walked away, he added, "Trust me and follow your schedule. Every day, every week for the next three years."

Later that summer, my coach explained that my whole training program was based on my personal minimum effective dose. What was the minimum effort at a specific training in a specific period? I never spent a lot of time trying to understand all these details. My training team figured out the best minimum effective dose and the consistency I needed. I trusted my team and did what I had to do. This well-thought-out program consisting of all kinds of training over a period of time would create results.

SPACED REPETITION

Ebbinghaus introduced one more technique: spaced training or spaced repetition. Spaced repetition suggests that your learners learn better when they space out studying over a long period of time. It would be better for a learner to review training materials once a week for five weeks than to cram in five short review periods over the course of one or two days. Isn't that exactly what my coach told me in 1989?

Additionally, Peter C. Brown, Mark A. McDaniel, and Henry L. Roediger III explain the key neurological principle of retention in their book *Make It Stick: The Science of Successful Learning*. As they state, the key neurological principle of retention is purposeful recollection over set intervals of time. Spaced repetition, then, is one of the tactics that can be used to create retention.

If you are convinced that a reinforcement program consists of a series of well-balanced communication moments strategically designed, delivered, and timed to drive business impact and lasting behavior change, you are ready for the next step.

STARTING WITH GOALS AND OBJECTIVES

To set up your messages properly and create behavior change, it's important to have a clear starting point. What do you use to determine your messages? Training goals or reinforcement objectives?

If you take a closer look at training goals and at how many companies describe these in their workbooks or on their websites, you will find lots of similar descriptions. Virtually no exceptions. I have seen many training goals in the last 12 years, and I bet you recognize them: "After the training the learner will be able to. . . ."

Imagine if my coach had used the same description for my Olympic program: "Anthonie, after the program you will be able to throw the Japanese Judo player on his back to win the fight."

If you focus on the verb in this training goal, you will find something strange. "You *will be able to*." It doesn't matter whether you do it or not, but at least after the program you will be able to do it! There is no Olympic program with this training goal. You don't win a gold medal just by "being able to." You must do it, use it, apply it.

After many discussions with people who are responsible for the design of training, I understood the use of the verb "be able to." They told me repeatedly that they cannot control what happens after the training. It's the responsibility of the learner, the manager, and the organization. "We did our part and brought them to the level of being able to." Is that the difference between a training program and a reinforcement program?

The difference between a training goal and a reinforcement objective is the verb. A reinforcement objective needs an active verb to determine your series of messages. A reinforcement objective focuses on the behavior you would like to observe in your learners. What specific behavior do you want to see that creates impact in your organization? I'll bet it's more than "the learner will be able to."

At the end of this chapter, I have included a 10-step approach for how to determine your reinforcement objectives based on your training goals.

The Importance of Verbs

Starting with the design of your reinforcement program, the verb in your objective is important. It determines the series of messages you want to impart based on the Forgetting Curve, spaced learning, and reinforcement principles. To create that series, a verb is essential.

I will give you an example. There is a big difference between a series of messages for the verb "use" and the verb "recognize." If you want to build a series of messages that address the verb "recognize," you can show different images and figure out whether the learners recognize the correct one; you can ask questions to see whether they know the specific features; and so forth. For the verb "use," you will have completely different messages.

When you select verbs for your reinforcement program, always look for verbs with an action that you can measure. "Use," "recognize," "write," "give," and others are good verbs to use. Avoid verbs like "remember," "consider," or "be able to."

If you want to select the correct verb for your reinforcement program goal, the definition of the desired behavior will help you a lot. Challenge yourself and your team to answer the next question without any doubts: "What specific behavior creates impact?" Discuss this question with key stakeholders to discover what the right reinforcement objective should be. To select the correct behavior and the appropriate verb, use the following six questions:

1. Why is this behavior important?
2. What do learners need to do?
3. What negative consequences could there be if learners do not adopt this behavior?
4. How will learners know when they are doing something right?
5. What would it look like to get this wrong?
6. What actions or beliefs cause the most problems daily? Why?

The verb should describe the behavior needed to create impact in your organization. Avoid verbs that don't convey action and are unable to show measurable results. Look at these examples of verbs that are hard to measure and do not have actions in them:

- "Think about the modules."
- "Consider different options."
- "Own the project."
- "Believe in yourself."
- "Know all procedures."
- "To be able to . . ."

Narrowing the Focus

Developers of reinforcement programs often start with an objective that is too broad.

I spoke with people in a big international sales company with lots of sales teams and managers. Their L&D department understood the power of reinforcement and invited me to their headquarters in New York. They showed me their training curriculum and explained the process they completed as a team to determine the needed behavior change. They had done a good job but needed some guidance to determine the reinforcement objectives. The showed me one of their outcomes: "Our learners use their management skills effectively."

They were right that their managers did not use the management skills effectively at that point. They were also right that an effective use of the management skills should be the outcome of the reinforcement program.

Although they were right, they could not determine a verb for their reinforcement objectives. I told them their objective was too broad, too general. Besides choosing the correct verb, it's also important to describe the behavior as specifically as possible. Instead of using something like "management skills," challenge yourself and make it specific.

Some good examples:

- "Use the four steps of delegation."
- "Ask open questions during their conversations."
- "Reflect after every team meeting."
- "Give feedback to the learner."
- "Listen first before they answer."
- "Spend at least 15 minutes on coaching activities."
- "Write daily emails to their customers."
- "Walk to their learners instead of sending emails."
- "Visit two vendors every month."
- "Talk to at least two stakeholders of a new project per week."

When you select your verbs for a reinforcement objective, a good check is to determine whether that verb is an action.

- Is your verb an action?

The verb should drive the needed behavior change. If you are convinced that you selected the right verb, use the final check.

- Can you measure the action?

If you can answer yes to both questions, you can start building your series of messages.

CREATING REINFORCEMENT OBJECTIVES

When you want to determine your reinforcement objective, use active, measurable verbs. By this point in the book, you should be able to create your own reinforcement objective. But just because you are able to create a reinforcement objective does not mean you are doing it. Use the following 10-step approach and determine your effective reinforcement objectives.

Before you start, I want to emphasize that a strong reinforcement objective will guide you while you are designing the messages in your reinforcement program. Actually, you cannot build a reinforcement program without an objective.

Step 1: Identify Your Top Three Training Goals

Earlier in the chapter, I explained the main differences between training goals and reinforcement objectives. Before you identify your reinforcement objectives, review your training goals.

To check or define your training goals, fill in the blank and be specific about each goal. For example, "After training ends, learners should be able to _____."

Now list your training goals in order of priority and identify your top three.

Step 2: Determine Desired Training Impact

Review your training goals to determine the desired impact. Here are some questions to inspire you:

- What problem are you trying to solve?
- What impact would you like to see in your organization if each of your training goals were achieved?
- What behavior change do you want to see from each of your learners?
- How will your learners apply this behavior change back on the job?

(continued)

(continued)

Next to each of your training goals, note the desired behavior change and the desired impact on your organization. Again, be as specific as possible.

Step 3: Measure Your Training Goals

Now that you have established your training goals, determined the desired impact, and explained how achieving each goal will benefit your organization, it's time to outline your measurement plan.

- How will you determine whether your training goals have been achieved?
- How will you decide whether learners are applying their new knowledge and skills?
- How will you determine whether your learners have achieved the desired behavior change?
- How will you measure whether the training was a success?
- How will you determine failure?

List your questions so you can collect valuable information about applying new knowledge and skills.

Step 4: Outline Reinforcement Objectives

Reinforcement objectives should build upon training goals to ensure application. Use the first three steps to build on your training goals and outline reinforcement objectives.

Reinforcement objectives should differ from training goals because the focus should be on application. Your learners have to do something or use a skill to prove that they are changing their behaviors over time. The desired behavior change should be clearly defined and measured by learners moving from points A to B.

Step 5: Include Measurable Action Verbs

With reinforcement, the focus shifts from knowing how to do something toward a more sophisticated model of evaluation, application, and mastery. Verbs accompanying the reinforcement model should include "do," "use," "master," "evaluate," and "analyze."

Review your reinforcement objectives again to check the verbs used for each objective. Do the verbs you used describe measurable actions? You may need to tweak the wording of your reinforcement objectives.

Step 6: Determine Key Takeaways

What do you want learners to take away from your training? Do you want your learners to leave with a new model of behavior or a new set of skills? Review each of your reinforcement objectives to ensure that they build upon your training goals.

- Are your objectives focusing on achieving the desired behavioral change?
- Is each reinforcement objective measurable?
- Will each reinforcement objective drive the desired impact in the organization?

Step 7: Outline Measurement Plan

You have determined what behavior change is needed to create the desired impact on your organization. You determined the desired behavior change for each of your reinforcement objectives. Now it's time to decide an allotted amount of time to achieve each desired change.

How will you determine success? Look at each objective to decide what progress you need to see and by when.

- What progress do you need to see from your learners and over what time period?
- What would you like to see after each month?
- What improvements would you like to see and when?
- How will you measure this?

(continued)

(continued)

Step 8: Close the Knowledge Gap

Review each of your reinforcement objectives to confirm they address and close the knowledge gap.

- What information or knowledge is needed to achieve each of your objectives? At what point in time?
- How did you provide your learners with this new knowledge?
- Do they understand all the information?
- Did your learners receive the necessary information during your training?
- Is the information given to your learners sufficient enough to achieve your desired impact and begin to change their behaviors?

Step 9: Close the Skill Gap

Review each of your reinforcement objectives to determine whether each objective addresses the skill gap.

- What skills are needed to achieve the desired behavioral change?
- Do your learners have the skills needed to meet each of your objectives?
- Did your learners receive training on how to master the skill and apply the skill back on the job?
- Do your learners know how to apply each of the skills?
- Are your reinforcement objectives focused on the skills taught during training?

Step 10: Motivate Your Learners

Do your reinforcement objectives address and close the motivation gap? Review your objectives to ensure your learners are motivated to achieve each of them. There are many motivation factors to consider, such as timing or number of objectives.

Has there been enough time for the learners to apply what they learned? Expecting your learners to change behavior within a few weeks is not realistic. Also, the number of objectives could overwhelm the learners. Expecting several changes at once could limit results. We recommend working on one objective per every five or six weeks.

Checklist

If you've successfully completed all 10 steps and finalized your reinforcement objectives, you are ready to move forward with building your reinforcement program. Did you complete all 10 steps?

Step	Steps to Determine Reinforcement Objective	Check
1	Identify your top three training goals	☐
2	Determine desired training impact	☐
3	Measure your training goals	☐
4	Outline reinforcement objectives	☐
5	Include measurable action verbs	☐
6	Determine key takeaways	☐
7	Outline measurement plan	☐
8	Close the knowledge gap	☐
9	Close the skill gap	☐
10	Motivate your learners	☐

CHAPTER 4

Influencing Behavior Change

Your objectives are ready! It's time to create your reinforcement program, build a solid foundation, and engage your learners.

The 7 Principles of Reinforcement will help you to create your reinforcement program. Your program will address all 3 phases of behavior change, emphasize the preconditions, and include all measurements needed to create actionable intelligence. You will drive the learners' engagement through a perfect balance of sending information and collecting data, giving direction and creating friction in their brains, and challenging your learners.

LEARNING THE VALUE OF REPETITION

I cannot remember whether my coach shared in an early stage the reinforcement objectives from my Olympic program. What I do remember are the days that I went to the dojo before going to school. Every day at 5:30 a.m. my repetition started. In Judo the movements of your feet are crucial. If your feet are placed correctly, your body will follow. My coach told me to do three steps: 1–2–3. I had to repeat every step 1–2–3 in front of a mirror. I looked in the mirror and worked on perfection. "Every inch counts," my coach repeated over and over again.

After two months, he came to me and said, "Now you are ready for it."

I was happy because it was wintertime in Holland and cold with snow and ice. I told my coach and he looked at me.

"You are ready for the next step," he said. He gave me the key to the dojo and said, "You don't need me for these morning sessions. Just repeat the three steps every day and do it faster. But keep in mind, it's not the speed—it's the quality *and* the speed. Create a reflex!"

And for the next several years, my brother and I repeated those three steps thousands of times every day.

I figured out that the basis of behavior change is repetition. Repeat a thing in training until it is etched in your memory or, as our coach always said, "marked in your mind."

The Value of Variety

Effective reinforcement not only focuses on repetition, but also incorporates various methods of presenting the same material different ways. Without variety, repetition loses value. Timing, length, and delivery played a vital role in my athletic training. Although my coach had taught the same lessons for many years, he always presented them in different ways and at different times.

Besides my feet, my right hand was also important. I specialized in a standing throw called Tai Otoshi, literally, "body drop." Without trying to make you a Judo specialist, understand that it makes a huge difference if your little finger points to the ground or points 90 degrees up to the right. It's only a couple of inches, but believe me, it can be the difference between winning and losing.

How many times do you think my coach told me during my career: "Turn your hand"? I would guess ten thousand times.

Imagine that he never changed the way he told me to turn my hand. I probably would not have heard his coaching anymore, or it would have had no effect. So my coach used a lot of variations to make sure I was turning my hand during the competition. Sometimes he just told me to do it; sometimes he asked me a question about how I turned my hand; sometimes he asked me why I did not succeed in my Tai Otoshi.

A photographer was part of the Judo team the day we went to the world championships in Belgrade. We were at the airport, and my coach introduced me to the photographer. I thought he was part of the campaign working toward the Olympic Games. After the tournament, my coach showed me the pictures the photographer had taken. They were all of my right hand.

In reinforcement, varying the message is important as well. You don't want to lose the attention of your learners.

SENDING THE RIGHT MESSAGE

The best coaches also strive to provide the right message at the right time. When I was 12 years old and Kees was 10, our coach did not give us the detailed advice needed to become an Olympic champion. He provided exactly what was needed for two young kids who loved to play Judo. Although my coach saw lots of elements that we needed to improve, his quality as a coach was in what he didn't mention.

If you want to change behavior, it's not about providing as much information as possible; it's about what messages you send at what time. If you guide behavior change, you are aware of the different phases of change. As you know from Chapter 3, there are 3 phases to consider. Each phase needs different messages. Ebbinghaus reveals the importance of including valuable information to increase the strength of memory. If you want to help your learners change their behavior, challenge yourself by asking: "Is all of the information needed at this moment?" Keep in mind that less is more!

If you consider that a reinforcement program consists of sending a series of well-balanced push-and-pull communication moments that are strategically designed, scheduled, and delivered, you have all the possibilities to facilitate the behavior change over time.

CONSIDERING THE ENVIRONMENT

After you determine what information is needed at what phase, take a look at areas besides knowledge and skills. To change their behavior, the learners' environment and motivation are just as important as their knowledge and skills. In the information you send, emphasize the importance of the environment. Is the learner able to practice? Does the learner have enough time, support, and possibilities to use the new knowledge and skills? What about support from the manager? Does the learner receive feedback? How is the reflection organized?

When I think back to the view out the window of that small hotel room, I remember only trees and snow as far as I could see. The hotel was in the middle of a forest close to Mátraháza, a village in northern Hungary. No luxury, no diversion, no acquaintances. Just 150 Judo players who gathered for a training camp.

Over the years, my coach figured out that this was the perfect environment for me to grow. I loved the back-to-nature feeling. No luxury gyms with clean and shiny fitness equipment. I needed tree stumps to carry through the mud, dirty and cold hands, abandon and pain. That was the environment that motivated me, one that inspired me to reflect and figure out what I needed to grow.

After a training session in the forest, the shower was a gift. After my hands and face were warm again, I was open for good conversations and reflection. It was the perfect condition to prepare myself to win the gold medal. Kees joined me one year. Although he did every training with full commitment, he hated that place. It was not his environment in which to grow.

TRACKING THE DATA

My team liked to measure everything. My coach always said, "If we do not measure, we don't know if we are on track. I don't want to spend a day going in the wrong direction."

We measured simple things like my weight, fat percentage, strength, agility, speed, condition, recovery—everything. All data was captured and analyzed. For some reason, I never felt all this measuring as "testing." I experienced it as part of my development and necessary for my growth.

All of my measurements were open and discussed. My staff explained what they analyzed, the conclusions, and how that translated into the next phase. Measurements became fun and an indispensable part of the foundation of my Olympic reinforcement program.

Tracking data has to be part of your reinforcement program. When you design your measurement plan, consider how and when to communicate the results to the learners. Avoid building a company assessment tool that only tracks data for your organization ("How many meetings did the learner attend?" "How does the learner rate the coaching of the manager?").

When you track the data, always think about what's in it for the learners. Remember, always add value for the learners. The learners need to answer questions that help them apply their learning and show more commitment. If you come up with good questions, you will collect valuable data for the learners and for the organization.

ENGAGING THROUGH ACTIONS AND REACTIONS

Once you build the foundation of your reinforcement program, it's important to keep the learners engaged. What drives engagement? How did my coach motivate me to continue 10 years of hard training?

Two hundred and fifty pounds! That is Yoshida, a Japanese Judo player's, weight. It was almost impossible to move that guy, let alone to throw him. While I lived in Japan, I saw him every day at the training facility. And every day he came to me and bowed, which means "Let's practice." He threw me so hard that every day was a nightmare.

I explained my frustrations to my coach. He just looked at me and said, "Use the principles of Judo, the perfect push and pull. Every action will give a reaction. So, if you push the guy, he will push back, or if you pull his body, he will react."

Using this Judo principle consistently was hard. I finally succeeded in feeling the effect of the perfect push and pull, but I still did not beat Yoshida.

"Use his reactions" was the answer my coach gave when I asked him why I did not beat Yoshida. "Don't focus only on your own actions. It's the combinations of your actions, his reactions and your follow-up actions."

Every time Yoshida made a bow, my coach whispered "250 pounds or not, use the perfect push and pull." Slowly my days become more fun. And after many weeks of practice, I succeeded. I start throwing Yoshida.

It's not the action that drives the impact; it's the combination of action and reaction.

If you compare this with your reinforcement training, the same principles apply. If you only *send* information to your learners, you don't know their reactions. Balance the information you send, ask questions to find out learners' knowledge level, create survey questions to understand their level of confidence, send additional content, and ask for reflection. The combination of sending and receiving makes a significant difference. So, create a series of messages that are well balanced, and use the push-and-pull principle.

THINKING THROUGH THE REASONS

If you think that I never argued with my coach, you are wrong. As I became older and more experienced, I knew what my body could do—how to train, how to avoid injuries, and what I needed to do to improve. My coach needed to give me less direction now compared with my early career.

Sometimes we argued about directions and what I needed to do and what was best for me. Sometimes I hated my coach and did not speak to him for days. I would ignore all of his advice and follow my own path.

My coach did not continue to argue about the direction. He avoided the "correct-incorrect" discussion. He started to change the training workouts. Instead of spending lots of time on the Judo mat, we went to the forest near where I lived. One day he parked his car and opened the trunk. I saw a brand-new big ax. "That's your new sparring partner," he said.

I picked up the ax, and we walked into the forest. We arrived at a place full of big tree trunks.

"Chop these tree trunks through the middle," he said.

"I am an Olympic Judo player, not a forester," I said.

"Chop!"

Completely confused, I started to chop. After three hours, I was finished. Without saying anything, my coach walked me back to his car, put the big ax back in his trunk, and drove back to the dojo. "Next week, same time," he said when I left his car.

The next few weeks were exactly the same. Without saying anything, we went to the forest and I chopped wood. I was irritated because my coach would not tell me why we were doing this training.

As time progressed, I found my own answer. Instead of being irritated, I tried to figure out why chopping wood had become part of my training. By analyzing the movement of chopping a tree trunk, I recognized that I was moving my body and arms in the exact same movements as I did during my favorite Judo technique. While chopping the tree trunks, I was programming my body and reinforcing my Judo techniques.

I was excited when I figured out the purpose of this forest training. I went to my coach and said, "I know why we use the big ax."

"I know," he said.

"But why didn't you explain this to me at the beginning?" I asked.

"Thinking about why you do something is sometimes more valuable than thinking of what you do," he said.

After he said these wise words about the why and the what, I began to recognize this approach more often. He gave me direction and created friction. No predictable workouts. The workouts I did were always engaging, and I enjoyed figuring out how certain training elements fit into my Olympic reinforcement program. My coach called this the principle of creating friction and direction. I cover this concept in more detail in Chapter 11.

TAKING ADVANTAGE OF THE OPPONENT'S POWER

After my success with Yoshida and chopping tree trunks, I started to learn more about principles. Within Japanese Judo, lots of principles are used. One of the principles is well known and explained by using an old oak as an example. Mister

Jigoro Kano, who created the Judo sport in 1882, explained the principle "use the power of your opponent" as follows:

> In a forest, there was an old oak with big heavy trunks. Around that old oak grew some little oak trees, nothing more than twigs. During one winter, it started to snow. The snow lasted for weeks, and the forest, including the oak trees, was covered by a thick layer of snow. The big trees held the heavy snow for weeks, but at a certain moment the big trunks broke because of the weight of all the snow.
>
> The little twigs were also covered with snow. They were flexible and bowed into almost a half-circle until their tops reached the ground. When the snow fell off, the twigs stood straight again. This continued throughout the winter. The snow did not get a grip on the small trees.

Kano used this principle to explain his idea about Judo. Use the power of your opponent. Don't be an old oak and try to be the strongest. Everybody in the Judo sport knows this principle and practices it during training.

THE POWER OF PRINCIPLES

A principle is a concept or value that guides your behavior or evaluation. It's a rule that must be or is almost always followed. In other words, a principle is an inevitable consequence of something, such as the laws observed in nature or the way a system is constructed. The principles of the Judo system are seen by all its users as the essential characteristics of Judo. They reflect the purpose of Kano's system; if any one of the principles were to be ignored, it would be impossible to effectively use the system.

A reinforcement system has principles as well. In fact, there are seven of them that you cannot ignore. The reinforcement principles are like lighthouses or natural laws that cannot be broken. These principles are not mysterious or specific to any sport. They are self-evident and can easily be validated by any individual.

These 7 Principles are proven to have enduring, permanent value. They're fundamental in building a successful reinforcement program. Although people may argue about how to define and use the principles, there seems to be an innate consciousness and awareness that they exist.

Part 2

BUILDING THE FOUNDATION

After your learners have been trained, you may think the work is finished. But truthfully, it's just started. To make sure your learners apply their training and achieve the outcomes you want, a reinforcement program is needed. A reinforcement program reminds your learners of what they were taught and how to apply their new knowledge and skills.

The three principles that your reinforcement program is built on are:

Principle 1: Master the 3 Phases of Behavior Change

Principle 2: Close the 5 Reinforcement Gaps

Principle 3: Create Measurable Behavior Change

CHAPTER 5

An Overview of The 7 Principles of Reinforcement

The 7 Principles of Reinforcement will help you to create a successful reinforcement program and a well-balanced series of messages. There is a strong cohesion among all of the principles. Some drive results by creating a strong foundation for your reinforcement program; others drive participation by focusing on engagement. Both results and participation are essential to making your reinforcement program successful.

This chapter explains how each principle influences a reinforcement program. Before you focus on the cohesion, let me list the principles:

1. Master the 3 Phases of Behavior Change.
2. Close the 5 Reinforcement Gaps.
3. Create Measurable Behavior Change.
4. Provide the Perfect Push and Pull.
5. Create Friction and Direction.
6. Follow the Reinforcement Flow.
7. Place the Learner in the Center.

PRINCIPLE 1: MASTER THE 3 PHASES OF BEHAVIOR CHANGE

If you want to change behaviors effectively, you cannot skip any of the 3 Phases of Behavior Change:

1. **Awareness:** Learners must understand *why* the behavior change is important to them.
2. **Knowledge/Skills:** Learners must know *how* to change their behavior.

3. **Apply:** Learners must focus on how to *apply* your training back on the job. In this final phase, learners should focus on using their newly mastered knowledge and skills in their daily work.

I cover these phases in more detail in Chapter 6.

PRINCIPLE 2: CLOSE THE 5 REINFORCEMENT GAPS

It is easy to determine the knowledge and skills your learners need for specific behaviors that will create business impact. However, to apply the new knowledge and skills, you need more. How is the environment to practice, to reflect, or know the options to fail? Think about my stay in Mátraháza in northern Hungary, with no luxury, no diversion, and no acquaintances. It was the perfect environment for me to learn.

What do you need to explain about workplace procedures? For example, perhaps you are a leader and the procedures for evaluating your direct reports are not clear. What will the results of the evaluations be? What will be the impact of your team evaluation? Even if your evaluation skills are fantastic, if your direct reports don't understand part of the process, they will not incorporate your feedback as well as they could.

If you want to change behavior that creates business impact, you must focus on all five gaps during your reinforcement program.

- **Knowledge:** Are the information and new knowledge sufficient?
- **Skill:** Do your learners know how to implement and apply their new knowledge?
- **Motivation:** Are learners motivated by internal or external forces to achieve the desired change?
- **Environment:** Do your learners have enough support and time to be successful?
- **Communication:** Do your learners receive enough directions, procedures, process, and other communication from you?

PRINCIPLE 3: CREATE MEASURABLE BEHAVIOR CHANGE

If you want to create measurable behavior change, you need a measurement plan. During my Olympic career, all sorts of measurements were taken of my body and of my performance. None of these measurements felt like assessment tools.

To create a foundation for your program, determine your objectives, which will determine the metrics you measure. Reinforcement starts with building on learning goals to determine the objectives. With reinforcement, the focus shifts away from knowing how to do something toward a more sophisticated model of evaluation, application, and mastery.

When you craft your measurement plan, think about the desired impact you want to see in your organization. Avoid measuring on a "happy sheet" level: "How was the training?" "How well did the trainer do?" "How did you like the workbook?"

When you design a measurement plan, consider how and when you will communicate results to the learners. Avoid building an assessment tool that only has value for the organization and not the learners.

PRINCIPLE 4: PROVIDE THE PERFECT PUSH AND PULL

If you want to maximize retention and drive behavior change among learners, you must provide the perfect balance between push and pull. It's not the action that drives the impact—it's the combination of action and reaction.

To deliver impactful reinforcement, think about the message you want to send and how to create the most impact for the learners. Also think about what the learners need to respond to you.

PRINCIPLE 5: CREATE FRICTION AND DIRECTION

To increase the impact of your reinforcement program, the brain needs to work. Lazy brains create lazy performance. You know how the brains works from Chapter 2, so you can optimize the effect for better results. In your reinforcement program, you need to find the balance between friction and direction, as my coach did with the big ax in his trunk.

You don't want to lose the learners because of too much friction, but also, you don't want to lose the learners because of too much direction or with a program that is too predictable. You want to find the balance between those worlds. When your learners' brains must work to master your content or complete a puzzle, or figure out the structure or connections, your content will stick much longer.

PRINCIPLE 6: FOLLOW THE REINFORCEMENT FLOW

Mihaly Csikszentmihalyi, a Hungarian psychologist, introduced "flow" theory in his book, *Flow: The Psychology of Optimal Experience*, which focuses on finding a balance between challenge and ability. According to Csikszentmihalyi, when a challenge far exceeds a learner's ability, it is probably too difficult and will frustrate the learner. On the other hand, when something is far too easy for the learners, they are not stimulated or engaged and the program is boring.

Most training experiences involve overwhelming the learners with a lot of new information. This leaves learners feeling exhausted. For your reinforcement program to be effective, check the program's structure and ensure that it follows the reinforcement flow.

Is your reinforcement program becoming more difficult to keep your learners in the flow, or is it just a reminder service? Keep a consistent balance between challenge and satisfaction to encourage engagement, retention, and adoption among your learners.

When Kees became Dutch champion, he was in the flow. All elements fit together. Ask any athlete who has won a medal and he or she will tell you the same thing: "I was in the flow."

PRINCIPLE 7: PLACE THE LEARNER IN THE CENTER

Reinforcement is intended to make a difference in performance, educate learners on how to do their jobs better, and promote the success and growth of learners. Many organizations focus on quizzing the learners, but keep in mind that a reinforcement program is not an assessment tool. Instead, focus on reinforcing and measuring the information that is most valuable to the learner.

Everything my coach, training team, and I did during my Olympic journey was focused on me. Everything—and I mean everything—was meant to help me perform as well as possible. No exceptions.

Sometimes it was hard for my staff to put my needs before theirs. My coach fired my physiotherapist because he wouldn't put me ahead of everything else. He was an independent therapist with his own company and clients. When I had a tournament, or came back from a training camp with an injury, my coach did not want to wait for the physiotherapist to see me the next day; he insisted on immediate treatment, even at 9 p.m. on a Sunday. The physiotherapist was not willing to make these sacrifices to his weekend. Although the therapist was good and understood Judo and its injuries, my coach decided to select another specialist who understood the principle of placing the learner first.

THE COHESION OF THE 7 PRINCIPLES OF REINFORCEMENT

To build an effective reinforcement program, your focus must be on results and participation. You cannot separate them. If you don't have focus on participation, your learners drop off after one week, and you won't get results. And if your program is not focused on results, you don't get much participation. Learners don't want to spend time on your program if they think they won't see any results. It's as simple as that. Even as a young sports person, I needed results; I needed to win some medals to stay engaged and motivated to train hard every week.

Supporting Results and Participation

Each of The 7 Principles supports results or participation. Three principles are needed to build a strong foundation to focus on results:

1. Master the 3 Phases of Behavior Change.
2. Close the 5 Reinforcement Gaps.
3. Create Measurable Behavior Change.

If your training foundation addresses the phases of behavior change, shores up the gaps that can lead to shortcomings, and identifies the correct measurements to analyze, it is built perfectly to gain results.

However, results require participation. The next three principles are more focused on engagement, which drives participation:

4. Provide the Perfect Push and Pull.
5. Create Friction and Direction.
6. Follow the Reinforcement Flow.

These principles help you stay focused on the engagement. Balance the actions and requested reactions from your learners, stimulate their thinking process without losing them, and make your reinforcement program more difficult over time.

But you are missing one principle:

7. Place the Learner in the Center.

Figure 5.1 depicts the relationships among The 7 Principles in terms of foundation, engagement, results, and participation. A bar, titled "7. Learner

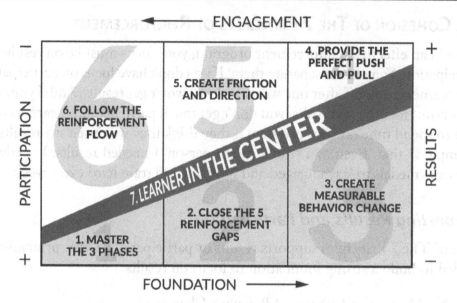

Figure 5.1.   How The 7 Reinforcement Principles Fit Together

in the Center," runs diagonally from the lower left to the upper right, across the first six principles. This bar is the Reinforcement Lever, which shows you exactly how well you do on the other six principles. If one principle is not used correctly, the lever will change position.

The three principles below the Reinforcement Lever build your foundation. As you know, a good foundation creates results. The three principles above the Reinforcement Lever drive your engagement. The better you fulfill each principle, the higher the results and your engagement will be.

Throughout the rest of the book, I help you fulfill each principle and show you what happens to the Reinforcement Lever if you fail. The useful assessments will help you to build a strong reinforcement program with great results and a high percentage of participation.

The Formula for Behavior Change

Before you learn about your foundation and engagement and the shape of your Reinforcement lever, I want to address the connection between those two. Do you know the formula for being effective? Effectiveness = Quality × Acceptance (E = Q × A).

I have seen this formula used in many consultancy companies that help their clients in all kind of change programs. If the quality of your message is perfect, but there is no acceptance, the effect is nil. As you know from math class, anything multiplied by zero equals zero.

If you want to be effective, you have to focus on *quality* and *acceptance*. The same goes for your reinforcement program. The quality is in your foundation, and the acceptance is in the engagement. Behavior Change = Foundation × Engagement:

$$BC = F \times E$$

If the quality of your foundation is 0, you won't achieve behavior change. If the engagement is poor or even 0, you won't get your desired behavior change.

Let's do some calculations:

Foundation	Engagement	Behavior Change
0	10	0
10	0	0
5	5	25
6	6	36
8	5	40
8	8	84

What does this overview teach you? Put your brain to work. Here's a hint: The behavior change is proportional to the improvements in your foundation and the engagement of your learners. Compare your conclusion with my findings over the last 12 years of developing reinforcement programs.

1. Never forget to pay attention to the foundation or engagement. Don't create a "0."

2. If your program is mediocre (the score is lower than 25) and you improve both your foundation *and* engagement, the behavior change will be enormous, more than three times as high (score 84).

3. Improve your foundation and engagement simultaneously. It's easier to create small improvements in both areas than a huge improvement in one area. The effect on the behavior change is almost the same: 6 × 6 = 36, compared with 8 × 5 = 40.

You will learn the details of how to use The 7 Principles in the following chapters. Each principle has its own principle assessment. When you use the assessment, you can see how you score and whether you need to improve. Each assessment shows an outcome that describes the suggested actions:

- Needs improvement.
- Needs attention.
- Good to go.

I offer you an assessment for each principle because this allows you to improve your reinforcement program with small and specific steps. When you combine the results from all of the assessments, you will have good insight about how well the foundation is focused on results and how engaged and willing to participate your learners are.

CHAPTER 6

Principle 1: Master the 3 Phases for Results

If you want to change any person's behavior, you must take into account that everyone goes through 3 phases on the way to achieving the new behavior (see Figure 6.1). First is the Awareness phase, then the Knowledge/Skills phase, and finally the Apply phase.

In the Awareness phase, your learners need to understand *why* it's important to change and *why* it's important to master new knowledge and skills. Once your learners understand *why* they have to change or use new knowledge and skills, they ask: "OK, I understand *why*, but *how* do I do that?"

The Knowledge and Skills phase starts now. In this phase, your learners need information about *how* to change their behavior or *how* to do things. After learners master this phase, you can expect that they can successfully work on their behavioral change by using the new knowledge and skills. This is the Apply phase.

If you skip any phase, your learners will not be successful in the long term. Just giving your learners new knowledge without a clear explanation of why they must learn it and why it's important in their daily lives doesn't make sense. And teaching only new skills and knowledge does not guarantee your learners will use it in their daily life. Before you can focus on the Apply phase and your learners can transfer learning into application, the first two phases cannot be skipped. You can change behavior, but you cannot change the order of the phases needed for behavioral change:

1. **Awareness.**
2. **Knowledge and Skills.**
3. **Apply.**

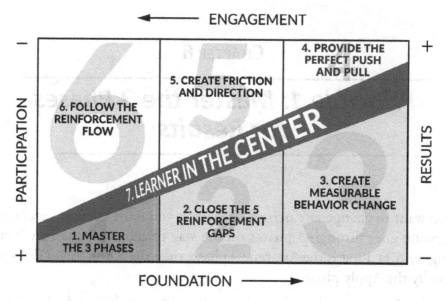

Figure 6.1. Master the 3 Phases

If you feel comfortable with the 3 phases of behavior change, it will be easier for you to select content. If you match the purpose of each phase to the message, the different medium or the type of messages is going to be correct.

WORKING ON AWARENESS

When you work on the design of the media and the messages for the Awareness phase of your reinforcement program, use the definition of awareness: the state of being conscious of something; understanding the "Why?" question.

While creating a program that will result in impact within your organization, ask yourself: "Does it help my learners answer the 'Why?' question?" Table 6.1 offers some examples.

Table 6.1. Answering the "Why?" Question

Good Examples	Not-So-Good Examples
Facts that show the impact of change	Learning elements (how to do it)
Graphs	Pitfalls
Quotes for inspiration	Assignments
Self-reflection	Explaining what is important
What-if statements	Knowledge checks

If your reinforcement program is based on a training event, your sources should be within the training materials, especially for the Awareness phase. Are you using mnemonics techniques? Recall from Chapter 2 that memories and emotions are produced and stored by different parts of the brain. The hippocampus produces and stores your memories, and your amygdala is responsible for your emotions.

If you use the same images, sayings, wordings, or expressions in the reinforcement program that were used in the training, your learners' hippocampus and amygdala work together to remember their feelings and emotions about the topic. In my analysis of many training programs over the years, I have noticed many of these techniques being used in the first part of a training, when the facilitator works on awareness and answers the learners' question: "Why do I need this training event?" Your use of the training materials in your reinforcement program will be effective and powerful.

ASSESSING KNOWLEDGE

Gaining knowledge does not automatically lead to behavioral change, although I agree that knowledge is needed for behavioral change. For that reason, the second phase is the "Knowledge and Skills phase." What is the right balance for your reinforcement program?

When you create a reinforcement program for behavior change, you can just check the knowledge level necessary. What is key for the learners to know for each objective? In the 10-step approach to determine a reinforcement objective, the eighth step focuses on the key knowledge needed. Normally, you don't need to ask a lot of knowledge questions; a reinforcement program is not an assessment tool. Creating good questions is time-consuming and not easy.

I have seen programs that require learners to answer 15 to 20 quiz questions, and then the platform shows the percentage correct and incorrect. Based on their scores, learners receive additional content to increase their knowledge about the content where they scored low. That is not reinforcement, but a mechanism to select specific training content.

As you build your foundation, don't mix a reinforcement program with a form of micro learning. I like them to be separate in the design phase, but combined while helping the learner grow. If your reinforcement program is aligned with the 3 phases of behavior change, a knowledge check is included. Is the knowledge level high enough to move forward to the Apply phase? Or is the knowledge level too low and blocking any successful behavior change? If the knowledge level is too low, you can offer the learners additional micro learning if needed for behavior change. Treat this as a separate program and an add-on to your reinforcement program focused on knowledge and assessments.

I mentioned the importance of a knowledge check before moving to the next phase. I have seen good results and a successful behavior change if the learner's score on questions answered correctly for key knowledge is 75 percent or higher.

APPLYING REINFORCEMENT WITH THE **DO-DID-GO** APPROACH

When you work on the Apply phase, your focus is on assignments, evaluations, and reflections. A proven approach is the "DO-DID-GO Approach," consisting of three connected reinforcement messages.

In the Apply phase, you ask your learners to *do* something. Of course, a specific assignment should be based on the verb in the reinforcement objective. It's important that this assignment be focused on the future. For example, "For the next week, you . . ." or "During the next two meetings, you . . ." or "In the next team meeting, you. . . ."

The second message is a *did* message, focused on the past. You ask the learners to look back and evaluate their performance on the reinforcement objective.

When you ask the learners to look back in the past, you increase the difficulty of the assignment. For example, "Last week we asked you to. . . . How did it go? Did you notice XYZ? For the next week, only focus on X." Or "In the last team meeting, you. . . . Did you use ABC? For the next team meeting, only focus on C."

DO-DID-GO

If you look at the structure of the *did* messages, you will see that they are based on the first meeting but have a specific focus. The second part of these messages is a new assignment based on the point just made.

The reason for a two-part message is simple: Not all learners will complete the first *do* assignment. It doesn't make sense to ask for self-reflection if the learners did not complete an assignment. So, you give the learners who "forgot" the first assignment a second chance. You honor the learners who completed the first assignment by making the second assignment more specific.

After the *do* and *did* messages, the learners are ready for the evaluation and self-reflection during the *go* message. You can decide what reflection you want to use. The learners should write down their findings in learning journals or complete their action plans or make an appointment with their leader to share their learning or complete a survey or write an answer to an open-ended question or evaluate their own performance in other ways. Always check any questions against your measurement plan.

KNOWING HOW LONG EACH PHASE SHOULD LAST

Another question that you may have while employing the first principle is: "How do you determine the length of each phase?"

It depends. If your reinforcement program is based on a training event, you can start with an analysis of that specific training. Check the training goals, look at your timetable, and analyze how the different topics are spread out over time. Your goal is to understand how much time is spent on each topic and why the program is designed as it is.

Check the exercises that the learners did during the training event and estimate the impact on the learners' brains. What was the structure, and what was the balance among awareness, learning, and applying? It is important to analyze the training event prior to building the foundation for reinforcement because:

- Reinforcement is *not* retraining.
- Reinforcement is *not* remembering.
- Reinforcement drives behavioral change.

Your reinforcement program drives behavioral change. If you create a retraining program or a reminder program, you can use the same proportions as were used in the training program. Reuse the training content and follow the structure of that training event.

If you create a reinforcement program based on a training event to drive behavior change, your understanding of that training event's structure is crucial. If the facilitator of the training event spent enough time and effort on awareness, you don't need to repeat all of that information in your reinforcement program. Or if the facilitator spent a lot of time on new knowledge and skills during the training event, you don't need to retrain the learners in your reinforcement program.

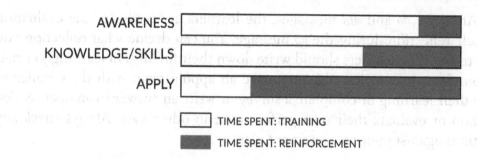

Figure 6.2. Time Spent in a Training Event vs. Time Spent in a Reinforcement Program by Phase of Behavioral Change

If you carefully consider the focus of the training event compared to the focus of your reinforcement program, your reinforcement program should be almost the opposite of the training event. In Figure 6.2 you see the time spent in a training event compared with the time spent in a reinforcement program per phase of behavior change.

Over the last decade, I have analyzed many reinforcement programs and have seen all the variations you can think of. The lazy program designers divide the content from a training event into small pieces and use a technical platform or their own learning management system to send this segmented content to the learners over time. That is not reinforcement. That is just sending out training content.

If the training event is well structured and the facilitator guides your learners according to the training event's established timetable, you can use the following balance of the 3 phases for your reinforcement training:

- 15 percent Awareness.
- 25 percent Knowledge and Skills.
- 60 percent Apply.

As you analyze the training event, you can adjust if needed. Be careful not to build an assessment tool or a retraining or recall program.

Necessary Repetition

In Chapter 1, I explained the 10,000-hour rule that I used to master my Judo moves on an Olympic level. That is four hours on every working day, 52 weeks per year for 10 years! That is more than behavior change—that is an Olympic metamorphosis.

To change behavior, some experts believe that material should be repeated at least 20 times before it starts to become a habit or starts to feel more comfortable and printed in our systems. Over the years, I have noticed that the time needed to repeat your training materials is influenced by the use of the 3 phases of behavior change. If, for example, you don't pay enough attention to the Awareness phase, 20 repetitions won't be enough. If you skip the Knowledge and Skills phase or ignore the 75 percent correctness rule, your learners will need many more repetitions before they can successfully change their behavior. Having said that, the way you design your foundation heavily depends on the structure of the training event.

Assuming that the structure of your training event is optimal and you master the 3 phases of behavior change, you need 20 repetitions per reinforcement objective. At least! Remember that your reinforcement objective is different from the training goal. Do you still know the difference between a training goal and a reinforcement objective? If you use the verb "are able to" for your reinforcement program after a training event, you probably don't need any repetitions.

> *One reinforcement objective needs 20 repetitions.*

If you combine the 3 phases and the needed repetitions or reinforcement messages, you can determine the average number of messages and their types per phase that you will need.

For one reinforcement objective, the breakdown is as follows:

- 15 percent of 20 repetitions is three messages for the Awareness phase.
- 25 percent of 20 repetitions is five messages for the Knowledge/Skills phase.
- 60 percent of 20 repetitions is twelve messages for the Apply phase.

If you want to determine the length of time for each phase, the level of intensity is important. How many messages can you send to the learners without irritating them? Even when the content is perfect and well aligned with the right phase of behavior change, you still can lose the learners because of too many or too few messages per week. Based on feedback from learners around the globe, two to three messages per week is an acceptable number and won't irritate your learners.

> *Send no more than two to three reinforcement messages per week.*

Determining the Intensity of Your Reinforcement

If you have one reinforcement objective, the average length of your foundation is easy to determine. Using 20 messages as a starting point and avoiding the irritation level by sending no more than two to three messages per week, a standard reinforcement program should be between seven and ten weeks long. If you want to increase the intensity of the reinforcement, you can do so in either of two ways:

- Shorten the number of weeks and send more messages per week.
- Add extra reinforcement objectives to the reinforcement program.

You can determine the intensity based on the target group. If you have senior leaders who travel a lot and spend their days in meetings, your reinforcement program may not be successful if you choose a high-intensity program. If you have young salespeople who have just started and are eager to learn, a low-intensity program with, for example, one message every two weeks will not be very successful.

Use the information in Table 6.2 to plan your message strategy:

Table 6.2.   Intensity of Messages

Level of Intensity	Number of Messages per Week
Low	1
Regular	2 to 3
High	4 to 6

Reinforcing Multiple Objectives

To increase the intensity, you can reinforce multiple objectives at the same time. How many reinforcement objectives can you combine in the same program? The question is "How many behavior changes can I achieve at the same time?"

As a kid, I liked sports very much, but it was impossible to learn how to ride horses, play ice hockey, do some Judo, improve my gymnastics, and increase my football skills in one year. So, there is a limit.

A simple four-step approach will help you to pick the number of reinforcement objectives in an effective foundation:

- **Step 1:** Determine the length of your reinforcement program (L).
- **Step 2:** Select the intensity (I).

- **Step 3:** Calculate the number of reinforcement messages (L × I).
- **Step 4:** Determine your number of reinforcement objectives (L × I)/20 repetitions.

If you want a three-month-long program (12 weeks) with a regular intensity (two or three messages per week) the four-step approach gives you the following:

- **Step 1:** L = 12 weeks.
- **Step 2:** I = 2 to 3 messages.
- **Step 3:** Total = 12 × 3 = 36.
- **Step 4:** Number of objectives: 36 messages/20 repetitions = 1.8, rounded to **two objectives.**

If you change the length or intensity in this four-step approach, you can find the right number of reinforcement objectives to focus on.

Focusing on two objectives in three months is a rule of thumb.

I will give you another example. If you have a period of four weeks and want to offer a program with a high intensity, the four-step approach shows:

- **Step 1:** L = 4 weeks.
- **Step 2:** I = 5 to 6 messages.
- **Step 3:** Total messages = 4 × 6 = 24.
- **Step 4:** Number of objectives = 24 messages/20 repetitions = 1.2, rounded to **one objective.**

Here's what the numbers look like for a four-week period and a low-intensity program.

Step 1: L = 4 weeks.

Step 2: I = 1 message.

Step 3: Total messages = 4 × 1 = 4.

Step 4: Number of objectives = 4 messages/20 repetitions = **0.2 objectives.**

Is the outcome unusable? No, but it is an indication that you will not reach behavior change with these settings. The score should be one or higher. See the outcome only as an indication; you still need to think as a professional designer.

EVEN A LOSS IS A WIN

If you compare sports tournaments with your role as a reinforcement specialist, what similarities do you see? When I was an athlete, I saw all tournaments as indispensable reflection moments. Of course, I wanted to win the gold medal for every tournament. But looking back at my sports career, I lost more tournaments than I won. As my coach always told me after I had lost a tournament, "You learn more from the tournaments you lose." (And then he probably added in his mind, "If you analyze the loss correctly.")

You cannot lose going to a tournament. Either you win a medal and receive a confirmation that the way you trained was good, or you analyze your loss to gain valuable insights about where to improve. I never had this view when I was a top athlete; I was disappointed by every loss. During my growth period, I went to lots of tournaments and hardly won a match, but that was not a reason to skip tournaments. I learned from every reflection.

I have created some small "principle tournaments." Challenge yourself in this assessment and see whether you win a medal or gain valuable insights about where you need to improve. Don't skip this assessment.

PRINCIPLE 1. ASSESSMENT

How did the foundation of your reinforcement program perform? Read each statement below and give yourself points based on the scale:

> **Poor:** 1 point
> **Fair:** 2 points
> **Good:** 3 points
> **Excellent:** 4 points

Principle 1: Master the 3 Phases

The ratio is 15 percent Awareness; 25 percent Knowledge and Skills; 60 percent Apply.	
Awareness is focused on *why*.	

Knowledge/Skills are focused on *how*.	
Apply is focused on the DO-DID-GO approach.	
Apply is focused on the verb in the reinforcement objective.	
An average of twenty messages per objective.	
Total Score:	

(A copy of this assessment is in the Appendix at the back of this book.)

If your total score is:

Less than 11 points: Needs improvement

11 to 16 points: Needs attention

17 to 24 points: Good to go

How well did you score? Did you win a gold medal, or do you need to improve on this principle for the foundation?

Remember the formula $BC = F \times E$. Look at your score, and determine the first small improvements you can make.

If you scored in the "Needs attention" category, you win the bronze medal. It is OK, but you are not there yet. Don't think that winning a bronze medal is almost the same as winning a gold medal. As my coach explained to me, "You did not win the bronze medal, you lost your gold."

If your score falls in the "Needs improvement" range, you did not win a medal. Your reinforcement program is headed in the right direction, but it's not good enough to create great results. Stay critical and remember what Kees told me: "To become a champion, you have to complete the smallest details extremely well."

CHAPTER 7

Principle 2: Close the 5 Reinforcement Gaps

If your reinforcement program addresses only the knowledge component and is focused on knowledge retention, your foundation is not strong enough to drive behavior change. This second principle will guide you to create a solid foundation that includes all of the elements needed for behavior change. Besides new knowledge and skills, you must also consider how the learners' motivation, or maybe better, demotivation, influences the results. Also think about the environment in which your learners need to grow, develop, and show behavioral change.

The 5 Reinforcement Gaps need your full attention while building your reinforcement foundation (see Figure 7.1). Focusing on each gap in turn will prevent you from building a weak foundation that cannot support lasting behavioral change.

OVERCOMING UNCERTAINTY

To understand the second principle, look at behavior change first. Change is never easy. We have discussed how the brain works, that is, instead of choosing the most beneficial solution, people place more value on the potential losses than on any benefits they may get from the unknown future. If you want your learners to change behavior, you're doing battle against the brain. Sometimes the battle is easy, but you should be prepared for difficult battles, too, just as in sports.

Reinforcement focuses on change.

You also know that learners can have either a fixed mindset or a growth mindset. Learners with a growth mindset like to take on more challenges and try new things, even if they may fail.

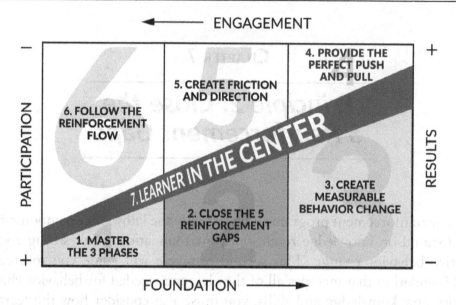

Figure 7.1.   Close the 5 Reinforcement Gaps

When you ask your learners to change their behavior, you ask them to leave a safe situation and move toward the unknown future. To prepare for this struggle, you need a solid foundation. New knowledge or an extra skill-set may be needed to move into a new future. We are talking about behavior *change*.

A reinforcement program guides your learners to embrace and function well in the new situation. Reinforcement is focused on the needed change, on the way to reach the future situation.

Changing behavior is different from strengthening current behavior. To strengthen a learner's current behavior, additional knowledge or an extra skill-set may be sufficient. Using new knowledge and skill-sets to create impact within your organization results in behavior change. The learners transfer their learning into action.

> *Change is the transfer of learning into action.*

As a CEO from big pharmaceutical company once told me, "No change happens without strengthening the current situation, but strengthening the current situation doesn't mean you change."

The same idea applied to my Judo career. I spent many hours in the gym to complete my weight training, but it was a complete waste of my time and effort if I was not able to transfer the new muscle power into my Judo moves during the competition.

To guide change successfully, first think about why people do not change. What excuses have you heard from your learners who are not willing to change? I often hear excuses like:

- I don't know why I have to change.
- I don't know how to do it.
- It's not clear to me.
- Even when I do it, "they" never give feedback or appreciate it.
- *Another* change! It's the umpteenth.
- I can change, but the system is still based on old processes.
- I feel like I'm the only one who changes.

I'll bet you can come up with 10 more excuses your learners give for why they don't want to change. It doesn't mean they are negative; these excuses allow them to maintain the status quo.

While building the foundation of your reinforcement program, know that resistance to change is normal (natural), and you have to deal with it.

EXAMINING THE 5 GAPS

The five areas that influence behavioral change are:

1. Knowledge.
2. Skill.
3. Motivation.
4. Environment.
5. Communication.

When I was an Olympic athlete, my trainer used these five areas to create my reinforcement program. My coach was always asking me questions about my opponents. He started with simple questions like "Is he left- or right-handed?" "What is his favorite movement?" "How is his condition?" or "How often has he been injured?" In the beginning, as a 17-year-old boy, I just answered his questions as he asked them, most of the time with, "I don't know." My coach answered, "You have to."

Gathering Knowledge

In 1989 I was injured. I had back problems and could not train or compete. My coach came to me in January and told me that he had canceled all of my tournaments until September. Before I could react, he told me that the next nine months were the most important months toward my Olympic gold medal.

He gave me an enormous stack of papers with a square on each one. The squares were exactly the size of a Judo mat. He told me that I would go to every tournament and watch all competitors from the stands. He gave me instructions to note every attack and the timing. When a judoka attacked, I needed to indicate where and at what moment.

I started doing this during the first tournament in Paris; I did not understand why I was doing it—I just did it. Over the next months, I started to see my competitors' patterns. My coach and I saw at what moment of the fight they attacked. An American guy was very active at the beginning and less active toward the end. The Russian judoka was only active and very dangerous in the last minute of each fight. We also realized that some judoka were trying new techniques or getting into better condition as 1992 approached.

I collected patterns from more than 80 competitors, and we built a database with this valuable knowledge. It was fantastic! We used all of this knowledge to plan our training strategy for the Olympics in 1992. My trainer closed the knowledge gap.

When you design your reinforcement program, you must consider the gaps in each learner's knowledge. Ask: "What knowledge is needed to successfully change this learner's behavior?"

My coach gave me the assignment to observe my opponents to gather new knowledge because this knowledge was needed for my success. When you design your program and select the reinforcement objective, determine exactly what knowledge is needed. What does each learner need to know?

Gaining Skills

The skills gap was closed during all my training hours, evaluations, reflections, tournaments, video analyses, and visits to Japan to attend a training camp.

In a reinforcement program, the skills needed for behavior change must be addressed. What skills are needed to change the learners' behavior? Focus only on the reinforcement objective and use the verb. What does each learner need to do or demonstrate once the change is implemented?

You know your learners best. Check gaps you see between their current skills level and the needed skills level. While you are designing your reinforcement program, add enough activities, demonstrations, and assignments to help the learners bridge the skills gap.

Finding Motivation

To close the motivation gap, or to avoid demotivation, remember the irritation level. Don't send too many reinforcement messages every week. Even when all of the messages are perfect, the messages you send must be valuable for your learners. My coach told me years after my career, "It was not hard to motivate you. It was harder to avoid demotivation."

Why do learners do the things they do? Why did Kees and I train so hard as athletes? What drives that behavior? Psychologists have proposed some different ways of thinking about motivation and demotivation, including looking at whether motivation arises from outside (extrinsic) or inside (intrinsic) the individual.

Extrinsic motivation

Extrinsic motivation is present when a learner is motivated to perform or engage in an activity to earn a reward or avoid punishment. In our case, we wanted to win a gold medal. In the corporate world, examples of behaviors that stem from extrinsic motivation include:

- Studying because you want a promotion.
- Cleaning your computer systems to avoid being reprimanded by your IT team.
- Competing in a learning game to win an incentive.
- Following a reinforcement program to create impact in the organization.

In each of these examples, the behavior is motivated by a desire to gain a reward or avoid an adverse outcome.

Intrinsic motivation

Intrinsic motivation means engaging in a behavior because it is personally rewarding; essentially, a person performs an activity for its own sake rather than for some external reward. In our case, Kees and I found all the different training activities super-enjoyable. In the corporate world, the results of intrinsic motivation include:

- Solving a project question because you find the challenge fun and exciting.
- Playing a game because you find it exciting or fun.
- Staying on track with a reinforcement program and enjoying the different messages.

In each of these instances, the person's behavior is motivated by an internal desire to participate in an activity for its own sake.

The primary difference between the two types of motivation is that extrinsic motivation arises from outside the learner while intrinsic motivation arises from within.

While you are designing your reinforcement program, think about your learners and address both types of motivation. What are the end goals? What can your learners achieve? and How can you drive the intrinsic motivation? In Part 3, "Building Engagement," you will read many helpful tips to drive motivation and avoid demotivation.

Considering the Environment

At an Olympic level, the environment gap is closed. Athletes have lots of opportunities to practice. More important is the support and time it takes to be successful. In your reinforcement program, you must give your learners enough time to work on an assignment or to evaluate it with their managers or their teams.

If you want to transfer learning into application, it is crucial to fill this gap and add to your foundation. Check your foundation. Did you answer the following questions:

- Does the learner feel encouraged by managers or peers?
- Is the environment conducive to learning?
- Is feedback addressed and communicated regularly?
- Is the DO-DID-GO approach being used?

Refining Communication

The first time I entered a big tournament, I was completely blocked. I was so impressed by the process to register as a participant, with the weigh-in procedures, with checking to make sure my Judo suit was not too short so my opponents could not get a good grip. I liked the transportation from the hotel to the arena. I loved the way the fighters were introduced to the public and hearing the official announcement that I represented The Netherlands. It was all new and unknown, and I liked everything about it.

However, none of that changed the way I competed. It was all the communication and the unknown procedures that blocked me. After competing at many world championships, the Olympic Games had the same effect. All of the procedures and communication during the biggest sporting event in the world were unique and more detailed and restricted than I was used to. It was overwhelming.

Are you communicating too much or not enough information? The last gap to look at is the Communication Gap: Do your learners receive enough directions, procedures, process, and so on?

It is important to transfer new behavior into an impact on your organization. For example, if a manager uses new behavior when evaluating his direct reports but doesn't know the correct procedures, his behavior doesn't have the impact it should have. Same for salespeople who are getting more or bigger deals; if they don't know how to proceed in their CSM system, it's worthless.

Some key questions to ask yourself while finishing your reinforcement foundation are

- Do learners fully understand all the information needed to be successful?
- Have you communicated instructions or procedures clearly?

This is the same as in top-level sports. All Olympic athletes are trained about procedures for talking to the press, attending the medal ceremony, warming up, and so on. It must be crystal clear how you are expected to perform.

EVALUATING THE GAPS

Use Table 7.1 to check whether your foundation is strong enough and covers all the areas needed for successful change. Make sure your reinforcement program has no gaps and that you have closed all five.

Table 7.1. Assessing Gaps in Your Reinforcement Program

Reinforcement Gap	Check Questions	Purpose of Questions
Knowledge Gap	• Is the information sufficient for demonstrating the new behavior? • How is additional knowledge (if needed) presented? • How do you check the knowledge level of learners? • Does the knowledge support the skills?	To check whether all knowledge required for behavior change is presented in the reinforcement program and whether the knowledge level can be determined.
Skills Gap	• Do your learners know how to implement and apply their new knowledge? • How have you organized the dependencies on skills level? • How did you present key skills versus additional skills?	To check whether all critical skills needed for the behavior change are addressed and not mixed with less important skills.
Motivation Gap	• Are learners motivated by internal or external forces to achieve the desired change? • What is their irritation level? • What elements influence demotivation?	To check whether the reinforcement program feeds the resistance to change.
Environmental Gap	• Do your learners have enough support and time to be successful? • How do you encourage social friction? • What feedback moments are included in the program?	To check whether your learners' environment has enough room for application, failure, support, and improvement.
Communication Gap	• Do your learners receive enough information about directions, procedures, and processes? Is that information clear?	To check whether the program provides all of the information needed for a successful implementation and adoption of new behavior.

Reinforcement Gap	Check Questions	Purpose of Questions
	• Do learners know how to maximize the impact of the new behavior within your organization? • What can block learners from a successful implementation of the new behavior? • How did you guarantee that the learners understand all the information needed to be successful?	

PRINCIPLE 2. ASSESSMENT

How well did you design the foundation of your reinforcement program? Read each statement below and give yourself points based on the following scale:

Poor: 1 point

Fair: 2 points

Good: 3 points

Excellent: 4 points

Principle 2: Close the 5 Reinforcement Gaps

The knowledge gap can be closed.	
There are opportunities for additional learning (adaptive learning, combination with micro learning).	
The skills gap can be closed.	
Scenarios are used to help the learners identify skills gaps.	
We know what motivates learners and how to avoid demotivation.	
We spend enough time on environment (practicing and asking for feedback).	
The reinforcement program creates enough time to practice.	
It is clear how the new behavior fits into the organization.	
Total Score:	

(continued)

(*continued*)

(You can find a copy of this assessment in the Appendix to this book.)

If your total score is:

Less than 14 points: Needs improvement

14 to 23 points: Needs attention

24 to 32 points: Good to go

How well did you score on this principle? Did you build a foundation that focuses on strengthening the current situation or a foundation that is headed toward a change in behavior?

Check whether you scored a Poor or Fair on one of the eight checkpoints in your assessment. Avoid Poor scores; those will not drive the change. One level up makes a huge difference. If you're critical now, you will be happy during the final analysis of the behavior change.

As Kees often says, "It's easy to become a champion, but it's hard to stay a champion for years." The same goes for behavior change. "It's easy to start the change, but guiding the change to maximum results is harder." Make sure your foundation facilitates the start of the behavior change and the continuation of it.

CHAPTER 8

Principle 3: Create Measurable Behavior Change

My coach's office desk was full of writing materials. The floor was covered with new training materials. Trophies and pictures of training camps and tournaments covered the walls. His office was a collection of many years living in the world of a top-level sport.

> *"Don't wait for something you already can measure."*
> —My coach, Koos Henneveld

My personal plan was scheduled on an old whiteboard. At one point, it showed 24 months until July 30, 1992. My coach had scheduled all of my measurements—speed, condition, strength, weight, fat percentage, knowledge of competitors—at certain milestones. My coach and I would discuss how I had changed my life to be an Olympic athlete: Did I feel comfortable with new skills? How well was I doing in my self-reflection? Had I grown as champion? Without using an assessment tool, he collected data to see when his interventions would be needed.

He always told the staff, "Don't wait for something you already can measure." He meant that every day counts. Why wait until the next tournament to figure out that my condition was not good enough? I agree. Why wait until the end of your reinforcement program to see whether it worked? Measurements are important, but the actions you take in response to these measurements will change the world.

As an Olympic athlete, I liked most of these measurements. How well did I grow? What skills had I mastered? How was I doing on my way toward my dream on July 30?

Of course, I hated some measurements. Although I knew they were good to have, I hated measuring my weight and fat percentages. They were a reflection on the way I lived the week before. I must admit, some weeks I did not live as an Olympic athlete, and my coach knew it the next week.

One of the things my coach always explained to his staff was, "If you measure at the perfect moment, each measurement is valuable. If you measure at the wrong moment, the outcome is worthless and your athlete is frustrated. So plan your measurements very carefully." And that is also what you must consider for your reinforcement program.

> *A good measurement at the perfect moment is valuable. A good measurement at the wrong moment is worthless.*

You have already created a strong foundation based on one or more reinforcement objectives. You used the first principle to focus on the 3 phases, and with the second principle you guaranteed the continuation of the change to close all five gaps. The last principle to build a strong foundation for your reinforcement program is to measure the behavior change (see Figure 8.1). When you use this principle, your reinforcement program will provide you continuous insights as to the learners' progress and behavioral change.

This third principle, "Create measurable behavior change," is a guide in how to use different types of measurements. You don't want to take a measurement at the start of your program and another at the end; if you do, you may

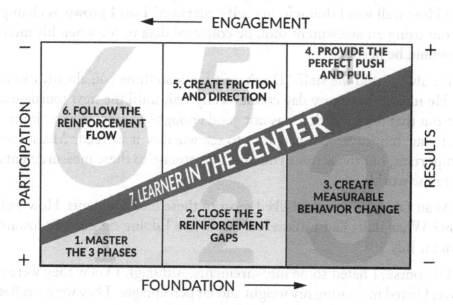

Figure 8.1.   Create Measurable Behavior Change

be rather surprised by the result. Furthermore, if you take measurements only at the start and end of the program, you won't have an opportunity to influence the result. With a solid measurement plan, you collect lots of valuable data, gain insights, and see the possibilities to use measurement throughout the program.

THE MEASUREMENT PLAN

When you put together your plan, start by measuring the current behavior and deciding on the needed change. Then you can decide how to measure the conditions along the way. Because behavior change is based on a reinforcement objective, create a separate measurement plan for each objective. As you organize the final training, you can merge your measurement plans.

In your plan, list the needed and observable behavior and the desired timing. Based on the reinforcement objective and the verb you selected, you can determine what behavior you want to see at certain points in the program to guarantee success. You must measure a lot more often than at a starting and ending point. Use the proof of the results of a training event plus the reinforcement program. But you should also measure progress during the program and use this data to create your interventions.

Behavior change takes time. Your learners need to practice and become comfortable with any new behaviors over time. New skills are mastered in small steps, and learners have to move through the 3 phases (why, how, apply).

When you applied the second principle, you closed the five gaps to ensure that change was not blocked. The process of behavior change challenges these gaps. Is one (or more) of the gaps "open" and blocking the learner from changing?

Know what you want to measure and when you want to measure it.

The first step is to determine what you want to measure and when. When you create the framework of your measurement plan, use the five What and When questions:

- What do your learners need to *do* at each point in your reinforcement program? (What mini steps will create the most impact?)
- What level of progress do you want to see from your learners and over what time period?

- What would you like to see your learners apply after one month? Another month?
- What impact would you like to see in the organization and when?
- What should the learners evaluate and reflect on and when?

If you want to check whether the framework of your measurement plan aligns with the behavior that is needed to create impact in your organization, use the reinforcement objectives. Use the thinking process and the outcome of the 10-step approach to determine a reinforcement objective.

Examine the preconditions for change.

After you have determined the points at which you want to see the defined behavior, it's time to determine the next measurements. These questions are not specific to the behavior change but focus on the important conditions:

- Do the learners understand why it's important to change?
- Is the needed knowledge on a correct level?
- Do the learners feel comfortable using new knowledge and skills?
- Does the environment still meet the requirements for growth?

The answers provide you with insight on how preconditions influence the learners' success. An important precondition is *knowledge*. I see that in almost every reinforcement program. Remember, increasing knowledge does not automatically mean using it. It is a precondition!

To determine the knowledge level, ask:

- At what point do your learners need to master new knowledge to make sure that a lack of knowledge is not blocking behavior change?

An important part of this question is: "At what point. . . ."

If your training event is well structured, your reinforcement program will consist of only 25 percent knowledge and skills checking. Reinforcement is not retraining or micro learning, so you only need to include knowledge and skills checkpoints if knowledge or skill level are preconditions.

Fine-tune your measurements.

It doesn't make sense to measure knowledge level as a precondition for successful behavior change at the end of your program or to measure the learners' awareness of the importance of behavior change after you check their knowledge levels. Follow the 3 phases of behavior change, collecting valuable data to use in your analysis and determining your interventions, as needed.

In practice, I have seen successful variations where measurements of the specific phases of behavior change are mixed. I often see designers who use knowledge measurements in the Apply phase to check current knowledge levels or to inspire learners to keep their knowledge levels up to date. I also see that designers use survey questions to measure the application of new knowledge and skills, not only in the Apply phase but also in the beginning of the program. In that case, the survey questions are meant to drive learners' awareness rather than to gain insights about how well the learning has transferred.

If you mix and match, your role as a reinforcement specialist will be challenged. You've already determined what you want to measure and when, so the final step to complete your measurement plan is the How questions. Challenge yourself with these questions:

- How will you ask the questions?
- How will you avoid being predictable?
- How flexible is your measurement plan?
- How can you avoid creating an assessment tool?
- How can you use connecting questions to determine progress?
- How can you balance push and pull in your reinforcement program?
- How will you create value for the learners and collect valuable data for yourself at the same time?

ACTIONABLE INTELLIGENCE

Using Principle 3, "Create Measurable Behavior Change," makes your reinforcement program results-driven. Once your measurement plan has been implemented, you will collect a great deal of data. How valuable is that data? and How can you optimize the results of your analyses? I would like to introduce Actionable Intelligence.

Before you learn how to use Actionable Intelligence, let's explore what it is. Figure 8.2 shows what to do with your data to take focused action within your organization.

1. During your reinforcement program, *data* is collected from carefully crafted and planned measurements. The first step is to organize this data.

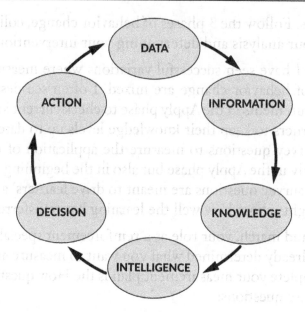

Figure 8.2.   Using Data to Take Focused Action

2. After you've organized the data, it can be converted to *information* in the form of reports or overviews.

3. This information can then be reviewed. The next step is to analyze the information to convert it into *knowledge*.

4. If you use this knowledge to predict why and what will happen, knowledge then becomes *intelligence*.

5. Based on this intelligence, you can identify potential *decisions*.

6. When you make a decision, you can define the needed *actions*.

But the cycle doesn't end there. It continues as you measure the results of these actions. Organize the data, convert it into information, and so on. This is how raw data from your measurement plan turns into actionable intelligence.

Measuring is so much more than just knowing.

Asking the right questions

During your reinforcement program, you want to gather as much data as possible. Apart from answering What, When, and How questions, you must also construct good questions. If you want to collect different data, you can use different types of questions. In Table 8.1, three types of questions often used in reinforcement programs are listed.

Table 8.1.   Types of Questions

Question type	Characteristics	Purpose
Quiz	The learners have multiple choices from which to select a correct answer.	Measure the knowledge level of the learners.
Survey	The learners have multiple choices from which to select an answer. These questions seem like quiz questions, but the difference is that every answer is correct. There are no correct/incorrect answers.	Help you to collect ideas, opinions, frequency, reflections, priority, levels of difficulty, or levels of comfort. In some cases, you may not be happy with certain answers, but that is different from an answer being incorrect.
Open-Field	The learner is not guided in the answers. After understanding the question, the learner is free to compile an answer.	Used for self-refection. The learner needs to think about the answer and write it down, which has a good effect on reinforcement results. If you limit the text box to 1,000 characters, the learners have to focus on the key points.

The difference between open-ended and closed questions

What's the difference between a closed question and an open-ended question? A closed question is one that can be properly and sensibly answered with a yes or no response. Closed questions always start with a verb.

- Are you using. . .?
- Did you meet. . .?
- Do you use these. . .?

An open-ended question cannot be answered with a simple yes or no. These questions start with W's and an H, as shown in Table 8.2.

Keep in mind that some open-ended questions are easy to answer, usually with only one word.

- Who. . .?
- Where. . ?
- When. . ?

Table 8.2.   Identifying Open-Ended Questions

Starters	Purpose
What	Event
Where, When	Situation
Which	Choice
Who	Person
Why	Reason
How	Means

Some reinforcement specialists consider closed questions "bad" and open questions good, but that is false. Each type has its uses. Closed questions, because they stimulate short yes/no answers are ideal for creating a fast-paced interaction between you and the learners. Clearly, closed questions are not ideal to stimulate in-depth thinking, which is a major function of open-ended questions.

Combining question types

If you combine question types, you can collect valuable data. What data do you collect if you, for example, combine a survey question and an open-field question?

You can ask the learners to answer a survey question about their comfort level using the new knowledge or skills. The learners must pick an answer from the four or five choices. The next question is an open-field question in which the learners are asked to explain why they choose an answer to the previous survey question.

By using this method, you can collect data on a macro level, but by following up with an open-field question, you also gather micro-level data. The coach can analyze the survey as well as the explanation from the learner. In practice, I see this combination a lot because it provides a lot of good insights on both macro and micro levels.

Think about what other question combinations would be powerful in a reinforcement program. Try these combinations in your program and analyze their value. After you are familiar with Principle 4, "Provide a Perfect Push and Pull," and Principle 6, "Follow the Reinforcement Flow," you will be able to balance your questions and avoid building a boring assessment tool.

Obtaining valuable answers

A good question generates valuable answers that can be analyzed. For a reinforcement program, one of my clients created a reinforcement objective, used the 10 steps, and followed all of the principles to build a strong foundation. The behavior change that the client wanted to see from their leaders was to have weekly meetings. To increase the quality of these meetings, the training event provided the learners with a form that listed the steps they had to follow to have an effective meeting. The survey question they used was simple: Have you had a meeting in the past week?

In Table 8.3, you see two sets of answer choices for this question. Which one would you select and why?

With answer set A, you collect the perfect data. X percent had a meeting and Y percent did not have a meeting. Answer set B gives you much more data:

- You can determine the number of leaders who had a meeting and did not have a meeting last week.
- You can determine from all the leaders who had a meeting and what percentage used the meeting form.
- You can determine from all leaders the percentage who had scheduled a meeting and who had not.

If you use survey questions to collect quantity data, I challenge you to add quality aspects. You will not only collect more valuable data for your purposes, but you will also focus the learners on quantity and quality. In a reinforcement process, the different answers influence the learners' thinking process. Don't create lazy brains!

Table 8.3.   Prompting Valuable Answers

Answer Set A	Answer Set B
• Yes	• Yes, and I used the meeting form.
• No	• Yes, but I did not use the meeting form.
	• No, but the meeting is scheduled.
	• No, the meeting has not been scheduled yet.

Don't miss an opportunity to collect additional valuable information. Principle 6, "Follow the Reinforcement Flow," will teach you how to use specific answers to balance skills and challenges.

Using ranges as answer choices

Using a Likert-type scale when you create the answers on your survey questions will also help you build actionable intelligence. The Likert scale is the most widely used approach to scaling responses. Some examples:

Level of Agreement

1 – Strongly disagree

2 – Disagree

3 – Neither agree or disagree

4 – Agree

5 – Strongly agree

Priority

1 – Not a priority

2 – Low priority

3 – Somewhat priority

4 – Neutral

5 – Moderate Priority

6 – High priority

7 – Essential priority

Frequency

1 – Never

2 – Rarely

3 – Sometimes

4 – Often

5 – Always

Level of Difficulty

1 – Very difficult

2 – Difficult

3 – Neutral

4 – Easy

5 – Very easy

Level of Quality

1 – Poor

2 – Fair

3 – Good

4 – Very good

5 – Excellent

Level of Comfort

1 – Not comfortable

2 – Somewhat comfortable

3 – Somewhat comfortable

4 – Very comfortable

Five common failures in questions

Apart from the improvements you can make to the answers, the question itself often needs extra attention. Review these five common failures in the design of a question before you write questions for your learners.

- **The question is too complex. Designers often write an introduction to the question, making the question unclear.**

    Example: Implication questions are sometimes important for ensuring a shared understanding of a problem's severity or urgency. As a result of well-focused implication questions, the customer articulates and thus sees the problem more clearly, along with the consequences of not addressing the problem. How confident are you in your ability to ask implication questions during a sales call?

    Tip: Split the introduction and the question clearly.

- **One question contains two questions.**

    Example: How confident are you in your ability to ask implication questions during a sales call, and what consequences does this have on your conversation partner?

    Tip: Have the learner answer one question at a time. Always!

- **The question is too vague.**

    Example: Sometimes confidence is important. How confident are you in your ability to ask lots of implication questions during most of your sales calls in the upcoming weeks?

    Tip: Don't use the words sometimes, some, many, most, several, really, good, lots, thing, very, big, a few, or enough.

- **The question could have multiple interpretations.**

    Example: How confident are you in your sales calls and ability to ask implication questions?

    Tip: Write out your question first, send it to a colleague, and then discuss it face-to-face to make sure there is no miscommunication. In this example, are you confident in the sales calls, or are you confident in the sales calls and asking implication questions?

- **The question is not personal enough; the learner does not recognize his or her own situation in the question.**

   Example: How would you rate your confidence level of asking some implication questions during the calls our salespeople have with our customers?

   Tip: Make every question specific to the learner's personal situation. Avoid words like the market, the customer, our salespeople. Later in this book you will learn how to write in the second person, and use *you* and *your* effectively.

If you avoid these five common mistakes in your design of the questions and combine quantity and quality in your answers, you collect the right data for your actionable intelligence.

PRINCIPLE 3. ASSESSMENT

For this last principle of the reinforcement program foundation, check how you performed when designing your foundation. Read each statement below and give yourself points based on the following scale:

     Poor: 1 point

     Fair: 2 points

     Good: 3 points

     Excellent: 4 points

Principle 3: Create Measurable Behavior Change

Clearly defined what progress is needed from learners over what period.	
Defined what results must be achieved monthly.	
Prioritized the improvements I wanted.	
Used a verb in each reinforcement objective for measurement purposes.	
Created the behavior change questions.	
Based measurements on important conditions needed for the behavior change.	
Based 25 percent on checking new knowledge and skills.	

Can convert reinforcement data into actionable intelligence.	
Able to find current issues and predict future ones.	
Will collect the right information about all types of learners.	
Used a Likert-type scale.	
Total score:	

(You can find a copy of this assessment in the Appendix in the back of this book.)

If your total score is:

Less than 20 points: Needs improvement

20 to 32 points: Needs attention

33 to 44 points: Good to go

How well did you score on this final foundation principle? How well did you complete the What, When, and How for your measurement plan? Look at the statements where you scored your design lower. Don't be too easy on yourself. A critical assessment is required for success. As they say, "Garbage in, garbage out."

CHAPTER 9

Recap of Building the Foundation

Before I explain Principles 4, 5, and 6, I want to recap the principles that help you to build a foundation. You need a strong foundation for your reinforcement program to achieve results. Read this recap carefully and make sure you have no questions before moving on to the engagement principles of your reinforcement program.

PRINCIPLE 1: MASTER THE 3 PHASES OF BEHAVIOR CHANGE

- Changing behavior goes through 3 phases:
    - The Awareness phase is the "why."
    - The Knowledge and Skills phase is the "how."
    - The Apply phase is "do it."
    You cannot skip a phase.

- Each phase has its own characteristics. Use mnemonics techniques and select specific media from the training event to remember content.

- In the Apply phase use the DO-DID-GO approach.

- Your reinforcement program is almost the opposite of the training event. Reinforcement is not retraining or a reminder program. It is a continuation of your training event.

- If you want a successful application of new knowledge, the score of the correctly answered knowledge questions per reinforcement objective must be 75 percent or higher.

- One reinforcement objective needs to be repeated 20 times.

- Irritation level = max two to three messages per week.

- The four-step approach will help you to indicate the number of reinforcement objectives within an effective foundation. (Length of the program (weeks) x Intensity (number of messages per week) /20 repetitions). As a rule of the thumb, two objectives in three months.

PRINCIPLE 2: CLOSE THE 5 REINFORCEMENT GAPS

- Reinforcement focuses on behavior change. The change is the transfer of learning into application.

- No change can happen without strengthening the current situation, but strengthening the current situation doesn't necessarily mean change.

- Use the check questions below to determine whether you closed the 5 Reinforcement Gaps, the five areas that influence the success of behavioral change.

Knowledge Gap

- ☐ Is the knowledge sufficient for the new behavior?

- ☐ How is additional knowledge (if needed) presented?

- ☐ How do you check the level of the key knowledge?

- ☐ Does the knowledge support the skills desired?

Skills Gap

- ☐ Do your learners know how to implement and apply their new knowledge?

- ☐ How do you organize the dependencies on a skills level?

- ☐ How did you structure key skills versus additional skills?

Motivation Gap

- ☐ Are learners motivated by internal or external forces to achieve the desired change?

- ☐ What is their irritation level?

- ☐ What elements influence their demotivation?

Environment Gap

- ☐ Do your learners have enough support and time to be successful?

- ☐ How did you encourage social friction?

- ☐ What feedback moments did you add in the program?

Communication Gap

- ☐ Did your learners receive enough and clear information about directions, procedures, and processes?

- ☐ How do learners know to maximize the impact of new behavior within your organization?

- ☐ What could block learners from a successful implementation of the new behavior?

- ☐ How did you guarantee that the learners fully understand all the information needed to be successful?

PRINCIPLE 3: CREATE MEASURABLE BEHAVIOR CHANGE

- Use the five "what and when questions" to create the framework for your measurement plan.

- Don't wait for something you already can measure.

- A good measurement at the perfect moment is valuable; a good measurement at the wrong moment is worthless.

- Use actionable intelligence to guide your learners in their behavior change.

- During your reinforcement program, data is being collected from carefully crafted and planned measurements.

- Use the six steps below to transfer data into actionable intelligence:
  - The first step is to organize the data.
  - After you've organized the data, it can be converted to information in the form of reports or overviews.
  - This information can then be reviewed and analyzed to convert it into knowledge.
  - If you use this knowledge to predict why and what will happen, knowledge then becomes intelligence.
  - Based on this intelligence, you can identify potential decisions to be made.
  - If you make a decision, you can define the needed actions.

- Measuring is so much more than just knowing.

- Combine the different question types to collect valuable data (quizzes, surveys, and open-field questions).

- If you use survey questions to collect quantity data, add quantity aspects in the answers. Don't create lazy brains!
- The five common failures in the design of a question are:
  - Too complex.
  - Two questions at the same time.
  - Too vague.
  - Possibility to interpret the question differently.
  - Not personal enough, so the learner does not recognize his or her own situation in the question.
- The use of a Likert-type scale when you determine the answers on your survey questions will also help you to build actionable intelligence.

Part 3

ENGAGEMENT

You can build a strong foundation with a perfect transition from one phase of behavior change to the next, lots of attention on the 5 Reinforcement Gaps, and an ideal measurement plan, but without participation, your reinforcement program won't create impact in your organization.

If you want to strengthen your reinforcement program, the next three principles will guide you. They focus on driving engagement. As engagement increases, the percentage of participation increases. Remember, the foundation creates results, and engagement creates participation. And both create impact in your organization.

The three principles that drive the engagement are:

Principle 4: Provide the Perfect Push and Pull

Principle 5: Create Friction and Direction

Principle 6: Follow the Reinforcement Flow

Principle 4: Provide the Perfect Push and Pull

"Provide the perfect push and pull" is a Judo saying. Judo is easy to describe, but hard for a layman to understand. I will try to explain to you what a perfect push and pull is.

In the old days, Japanese warriors wore heavy armor to protect them from being injured during their fights. A complete set of armor with helmet weighed 55 to 60 pounds. As long as you stood upright, it was good protection, but not if you fell during the fight and lay flat on your back. Because the armor was so heavy, you could not get up quickly, which often meant you lost the battle.

In modern Judo, the heavy armor has been replaced by a much lighter suit, called Judogi in Japanese. What has remained the same is that if you end up flat on your back—you lose. For that reason, Judo players all over the world practice throwing their opponents flat on their backs. If that happens, the referee says, "Ippons," which means "end of the fight." Over the years, I practiced my favorite Judo throw so many times that it became a reflex.

Another principle of Judo comes from an old Japanese sensei (teacher): "It is difficult to move a heavy rock, but once the rock is moving, it will take less energy." In Judo, we think of it this way: "It's easier to throw your opponent while he is moving." So, to become a Judo specialist, you need to move your opponent first, and while he is moving, you use your throwing technique.

Mister Jigoro Kano taught us to use the strength of our opponent against him. "If you push your opponent, you will get a reaction. If you pull your opponent, you will get a reaction. Find the balance between push and pull."

If you push your opponent's shoulders, you will get some resistance, which you can use for your Judo technique. If you pull on someone's Judogi sleeves, he will probably pull back, and you can use that power for your technique. Mister Kano explained this as "Action gives a reaction, and a reaction asks for the next action."

To use Judo techniques successfully, you continually have to push and pull your opponent. You use the power of the reactions you create. It's not only the Judo throwing technique that creates a result, but a combination between the throwing technique and the perfect push and pull.

That is exactly what you want to create in your reinforcement program. A good foundation (like the throwing techniques in the Judo world) is not enough. You need the perfect push and pull to "connect" with your learners.

PAIRING THE PRINCIPLES

If you compare the three principles you used to build your foundation with the three principles you will use to create engagement, you will see that:

- Building the foundation starts with the perfect balance of the 3 phases (Principle 1). Creating engagement starts with the balance between push and pull (Principle 4).
- Closing the five gaps (Principle 2) is required to have a solid foundation. Creating friction and direction (Principle 5) is required to let learners' brains work hard and drive involvement.
- To create measurable behavior change (Principle 3), you use your measurement plan to verify the performance. By following the reinforcement flow (Principle 6), you optimize learners' performance.

You can see the relationships among these principles in Figure 10.1.

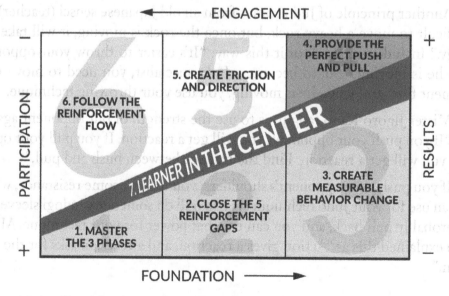

Figure 10.1.   Provide the Perfect Push and Pull

PUSHING THE BRAIN TO ENGAGE

If you take a closer look at Principle 4, "Provide the Perfect Push and Pull," you will see that an acceleration of the learners' growth cannot and will not occur if your learners are left to drive their own growth. One of the reasons is that the brain is lazy. More important is the relationship between memory and energy and the role that this relationship plays in learning.

The memory function of the brain allows your learners to update their knowledge and avoid mistakes. As you remember things, an ongoing energy dynamic occurs in your brain. However, your brain is extremely lazy. Before you judge your brain for its lack of motivation, realize that it's that way for a reason. Despite accounting for only about 2 percent of your body weight, it sucks up an average of 20 percent of your overall energy (as measured in calorie burn).

> *Your brain sucks up 20 percent of your overall energy.*

Because of this intense energy demand, your brain is always looking for shortcuts that will allow it to use less energy whenever possible. In the worst case, it won't even use shortcuts but simply will not spend any energy at all. For that reason, you constantly need to "push" your brain and avoid using shortcuts when learning new knowledge and skills. There are no shortcuts in top-level sports or when mastering new knowledge and skills.

The memory system helps the brain effectively use energy. When you offer learners a novel environment (mostly in the training events), their brains are active and absorbing information. They must *think* in those situations, which, in turn, generates memories that are easier to access during the reinforcement. Once the learners are around certain stimuli enough, their lazy brains start to mush those memories together and group them into a distinguishable collection.

A critical component of all this is that thinking hard *feels* difficult because your brain is fighting to stop you from using energy unnecessarily. Cognitive scientists talk about the difficulty in terms of *fluency* (easy thoughts) and *disfluency* (difficult thoughts).

That's why exposing ourselves to familiar environments and concepts is always more comfortable. We don't have to think hard (or at all) about them, and our brains remain calm because we don't have to worry about its precious energy going away.

When learning something new, everything will seem difficult and confusing at first, and the brain will fight back because it's blasting through energy it doesn't want to give away. But once a learner has been exposed to the new information frequently enough, everything starts to get easier. Even though the learner will still be a novice when this begins to happen, it will feel less and less like a chore to learn.

In your reinforcement role, you must understand and embrace the early disfluency (difficult thoughts) the learners will feel and push through until they reach a baseline level of fluency (easy thoughts). Once they reach that baseline, learning becomes progressively easier. You must stimulate their brains until learners reach the baseline level of fluency (easy thoughts). If you don't, the learners will drop off, and you will see no participation.

Before you try to use Principle 4, "Provide the Perfect Push and Pull," make sure you understand why brains need a push and pull and how to create memories via mnemonics techniques (visual or verbal) to activate the memory system. You can use mnemonics (visual or verbal) to activate the memory system. Reuse images, models, or phrases.

BALANCING PUSH WITH PULL

If you want to facilitate the learning process and accelerate learners' growth, you need to push and pull. This principle is all about the perfect balance between push and pull communication moments. If you send information to learners, it is considered a push communication. When you pull information, you ask the learners to do or evaluate something or answer your message. All the messages you send to the learners are push messages, but not all of your push results in a pull.

Not all of your push is a pull.

A simple push/pull example

If you have a reinforcement objective with an average of 20 repetitions, what percentage is push and what percentage is pull communication? Before you answer that question, look at some examples of the different push and pull messages in Table 10.1.

Table 10.1. Push and Pull Messages

Push	Pull
Learning messages	All types of questions to be answered
Video, PDF, image or audio file	Self-reflection
Pitfalls	Feedback (peer or coach)
Assignments	Assignment plus action plan

To answer the question, let's analyze the example in Table 10.2, which shows a proven reinforcement program, with one objective and 20 reinforcement messages (plus a welcome and a thank-you message). The example is based on a strong foundation and the perfect balance between push and pull.

Table 10.2. Series of Successful Push/Pull Messaging

Message Number	Push/ Pull	Explanation
1	Push	This is a welcome message.
		Explain what the program means to your learners and why they will be receiving messages from you. Avoid explaining logistics or length of the program. Focus on what's in it for the learners. Add your logo to emphasize company commitment.
2	Push	This message is to support awareness.
		Use facts and information that explain *why* this objective is important for your learners. Using graphs or images with statistics is a good idea. Make sure your learners can read the numbers and text in the image you upload.
3	Pull	This is an open-field question to create awareness.
		Have the learners think about why behavior change is important. What will the impact be in their daily lives? Use the introduction to the question as a learning moment.
4	Pull	This is a repeating survey question.
		The exact same question will be asked later in the program to collect data and analyze the difference in responses. To create this question, focus on exactly what you want to measure and what behavior you want to see.

(continued)

Table 10.2. *(Continued)*

Message Number	Push/ Pull	Explanation
5	Pull	This is the first knowledge check for this reinforcement objective.
		Provide the learners with instant feedback about whether their answers are correct or incorrect. The next three messages are knowledge checks, so start with an easy question. Let the learners feel the success of giving a correct answer.
6	Pull	This message is sent to the learner right after the learner completes the first knowledge question.
		Make the question more difficult than the previous one, but keep the focus on the objective.
7	Pull	After the knowledge checks, an important learning moment occurs.
		Make the question more difficult than the previous ones. Use different answer choices to make this question more challenging.
8	Pull	This is the last measurement of knowledge before your learners start the Apply phase.
		What is key that they need to know? Perhaps use a short scenario.
9	Push	This message is designed to recap all the knowledge needed.
		Attach media files and refer to training materials. Keep in mind that this message should help your learners answer *"How do I change my behavior?"* Consider addressing common pitfalls.
10	Pull	This message seeks to find out ideas or opinions from the learners.
		For example, "How comfortable are you with your current knowledge level?" Use a Likert-type scale.
11	Push	This is the first message of a series of five.
		Describe what your learners must *do* in the future. Give an assignment for the next few days.
12	Push	This message presents a new assignment.
		Make this one more specific. (The learners who did not do the first assignment will have a second chance before they need to evaluate.)

Message Number	Push/ Pull	Explanation
13	Push	In this message, you ask the learners to look back on their performance.
		"*How* did it go?" Learners are expected to look back and evaluate how they performed on the last two assignments. But don't measure yet. Ask them to think about improvements. Keep the focus on the reinforcement objective!
14	Pull	The previous message was a reflection without measurement. This message is a self-reported measurement of how well they did.
		For example, how often did they use the skills or how comfortable are they with their use? Use a Likert-type scale again.
15	Pull	This open-field question is related to the previous message.
		In this message you want to gather more insights on why the learners answered the previous survey the way they did. For example, "Please explain why you selected the answer you did on the previous question."
16	Push	With this message, you start a new series of three assignments.
		Give more difficult or more specific assignments. This message is an assignment for the next few days.
17	Push	This is similar to the previous series of assignments.
		Use a more specific assignment that will challenge your learners.
18	Push	Now question your learners.
		"*How* did they do?" Allow your learners to evaluate their performance and reflect on the assignments. Ask them to be honest and critical.
19	Pull	The next message is another open-field question.
		Use this open-field question to collect more insights from the learners' reflections.
20	Pull	This is a repeating survey question to measure behavior change.
		It is the exact same question as in the beginning of this series.
21	Push	Use this message as a recap of all learning and pitfalls to applying the new behavior.
		Use media or send a PDF file that refers to the training materials. Consider giving the learners an assignment to complete their action plans.

(continued)

Table 10.2. *(Continued)*

Message Number	Push/ Pull	Explanation
22	Push	This is the last message of your reinforcement program. Give your learners compliments and celebrate their accomplishments. Perhaps add a nice image visualizing celebration or completion. Share with the learners what happens next.

Principle 4 states, "Provide the Perfect Push and Pull." The perfect balance between push and pull is when your pull messages are between 40 and 65 percent of the total. In this example, 22 reinforcement messages are used to help your learners apply what they have learned. Of the 22 messages, 11 messages (50 percent) are pull messages.

> *In a perfect balance between push and pull, 40 to 65 percent of your messaging is pull.*

When you begin your reinforcement program, I recommend using a basic outline like the one in Table 10.2.

Creating a complex push/pull schedule

What would you do if you had two reinforcement objectives in the same 12-week period? The rule of thumb for reinforcing training is to focus on two objectives for every three months. For every extra objective, add another month. What would you do with push/pull messaging if you had three objectives and 16 weeks?

In Table 10.3, I've outlined a schedule for reinforcing two reinforcement objectives in 12 weeks. The table shows how many messages I send per week and on which day of the week. I start the reinforcement program on the Monday of the first week. You can also see what specific objective the reinforcement message is related to. Is it a push message or a pull? To help you with this outline, I included the message type.

In this example, 22 of the 42 messages—52 percent—are pull messages. This is a perfect application of Principle 4, "Provide the Perfect Push and Pull."

Table 10.3.   Schedule for Two Objectives Over Twelve Weeks

Week/Day	Objective	Push/Pull	Message Type
1/1	General	Push	Welcome to the program
1/1	1	Push	Learning element
1/3	1	Pull	Self-reflection with an open-field question
2/1	1	Pull	Behavior change question (Do they apply?)
2/3	1	Pull	Knowledge question (easy level)
2/3	1	Pull	Knowledge question (more difficult level)
3/2	1	Pull	Knowledge question (difficult level)
3/3	1	Pull	Knowledge question (key knowledge level)
3/5	1	Push	Learning/pitfall element
4/2	2	Push	Learning element
4/3	2	Pull	Self-reflection with an open-field question
4/3	2	Pull	Behavior change question (Do they apply?)
4/5	1	Pull	Survey question about progress
4/5	1	Push	Assignment
5/3	1	Push	Assignment/evaluation
6/1	1	Push	Assignment/evaluation
6/4	1	Pull	Survey question about progress
6/4	1	Pull	Self-reflection with an open-field question
7/1	2	Pull	Knowledge question (easy level)
7/1	2	Pull	Knowledge question (more difficult level)
7/3	2	Pull	Knowledge question (difficult level)
7/5	2	Pull	Knowledge question (key knowledge level)
7/5	2	Push	Learning element
8/1	2	Pull	Survey question about progress
8/1	2	Push	Assignment

(continued)

Table 10.3. (*Continued*)

Week/Day	Objective	Push/Pull	Message Type
8/4	2	Push	Assignment/evaluation
9/1	2	Push	Assignment/evaluation
9/3	2	Pull	Survey question about progress
9/3	2	Pull	Self-reflection with an open-field question
9/4	1	Push	Assignment
10/1	1	Push	Assignment/evaluation
10/3	1	Push	Assignment/evaluation
10/5	1	Pull	Self-reflection with an open-field question
10/5	1	Pull	Behavior change question (Do they apply?)
11/1	2	Push	Assignment
11/3	2	Push	Assignment/evaluation
11/5	2	Push	Assignment/evaluation
12/2	2	Pull	Self-reflection with an open-field question
12/2	2	Pull	Behavior change question (Do they apply?)
12/4	1	Push	Learning/pitfall element
12/4	2	Push	Learning/pitfall element
12/5	General	Push	Finish and Congratulations

Tracking your progress

If you want to check the progress of your reinforcement program, use the Pull Thermometer in Figure 10.2. Count all of the messages in your reinforcement program, and determine the percentage of pull messages (the messages that require an action from the learner via a question). Do not count the self-reflections without a question. Determine the number of pull messages divided by the number of total messages and add this percentage to the Pull Thermometer.

What is your percentage? Make sure you stay between 35 percent and 70 percent. I personally prefer to be in the range of 40 to 65 percent.

If your score is below 35 percent, your program is more like a micro learning module. That's good if that is your goal. However, for a reinforcement program, you need to create more interaction with the learners. This drives the engagement.

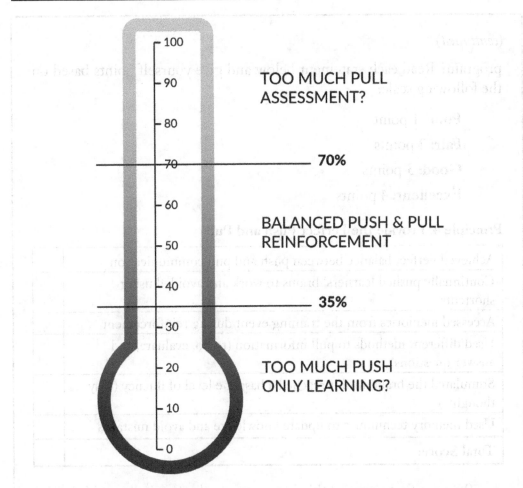

Figure 10.2. The Pull Thermometer Helps You Assess the Progress of Your Reinforcement Program

If your score is above 70 percent, you have a lot of pull messages, perhaps too many. Your reinforcement program leans more toward an assessment. Again, if that is the goal, it's perfect. But if your goal is to create a reinforcement program, you need to reduce the number of pull questions. Give the learners added value via learning and pitfalls. More assignments and evaluations increase the application of knowledge and skills as well as the engagement of your learners.

PRINCIPLE 4. ASSESSMENT

Continue assessing your implementation of the three principles that drive engagement. How did you perform in designing your reinforcement

(continued)

(*continued*)

program? Read each statement below and give yourself points based on the following scale:

Poor: 1 point

Fair: 2 points

Good: 3 points

Excellent: 4 points

Principle 4. Provide the Perfect Push and Pull

Achieved perfect balance between push and pull communication	
Continually pushed learners' brains to work and avoided using shortcuts	
Accessed memories from the training event during reinforcement	
Used different methods to pull information (to do, evaluate, and answer questions)	
Stimulated the brain until it reached a baseline level of fluency (easy thoughts)	
Used memory techniques to update knowledge and avoid mistakes	
Total Score:	

(You can find a copy of this assessment in the Appendix to this book.)

If your total score is:

Less than 12 points: Needs improvement

12 to 19 points: Needs attention

20 to 24 points: Good to go

How did you score on this principle? You will see a lot of improvement in your learners if you avoid retraining and focus on application and evaluation. Remember that each phase of the behavior change has its own approach. In the Knowledge and Skills phase, it's an art to test knowledge while at the same time supporting the learners.

CHAPTER 11

Principle 5: Create Friction and Direction

When I was the Dutch Judo champion in 1991, I prepared hard for the tournaments that led up to the European championship, which was held in May. Winning that tournament would be the first step toward my Olympic dream. If I won a medal, I would be selected for the Dutch Olympic team for Barcelona in 1992. After I was selected, I could prepare myself and fully focus on the games—no more selection tournaments and no uncertainties. I could spend every day in preparation for my performance on July 30, 1992.

In Holland I was the man to beat in my weight category. I felt strong, and self-confident and was ready for each competition prior to the European championship. It felt like an easy ride. I thought, "Let's do some tournaments in the spring, train hard like always, and focus on a medal in May."

No one else in Holland could block my road. "Nobody," I thought, "except my trainer." Looking back on that period, my trainer probably noticed this attitude.

In spring 1991, the Dutch national team participated in a selection tournament in Russia. The national Dutch team in Judo wasn't like a football team or an ice hockey team, where the players participate as a team. Judo athletes compete individually in different weight classes from bantam weight through heavyweight. (I competed in the light middleweight class.) We all traveled at the same time and wore the same outfit, orange, of course. The Dutch team met at Schiphol airport to travel to Russia. We always waited until everyone on the team was at the airport before checking in.

As always, Kees and I were some of the first to arrive. To kill time until everybody arrived, I was joking around with other team members when I saw someone I didn't want to be there. He was also a Judo player—the runner-up in my weight category. He joined the team, wore the same orange outfit as the rest of us, and checked in for the flight to Russia. I was upset and angry. I marched over to my coach and told him exactly how I felt about the other athlete's presence. I told my coach, "I don't trust you anymore."

During the three-and-a-half-hour flight to Russia, I did not say anything. My thoughts went wild.

When I checked into my room at the hotel, my anger and frustration switched to motivation. "Is that guy really thinking that he can block my Olympic dream?" I thought. "*No* way!" My whole body was alert and focused.

The competition started the next day at 7 a.m. with the weigh-in. At a Judo tournament, all Judo players (between 50 and 80 players per weight class) are weighed in the morning. If an athlete's weight is four ounces too heavy—less than a medium-size cup of coffee—the athlete is disqualified. I was the first one on the scale and qualified. I did a warm-up as never before, and every part of me—body and brain—was ready to perform.

At the end of the day, I won the silver medal. A Russian guy beat me in the finals. I must admit, he was stronger that day. This silver medal was a good measurement of where I was on my Olympic journey.

My archnemesis did well. He won three fights, which motivated me during the day to stay focused and alert. He lost his fourth fight and failed to move to the next round. His tournament was over, and I was in the final. Did I lose the final because I knew he couldn't beat me anymore? I'll never know, but I think that was the main reason.

After the tournament, my coach came to me, and we sat down on a wooden bench. "Are you still angry?" he asked. How could I be angry with a silver medal around my neck? Then he said slowly, "You needed friction to perform." He explained that he had been observing my behavior during the training leading up to that tournament. I was protected, felt safe, why worry? It was too easy. He needed my fire to return. I told him he took a risk. What would have happened if the other guy had won silver?

"I know what you think, and I know what I'm doing," was all he said.

The same is true for Principle 5, "Create Friction and Direction." If the learning is too easy, people are not motivated; if your learning event is too predictable, people don't stay motivated. If it's too clear what the reinforcement is about, their brains get lazy. When you create friction and direction, you must find a balance between the two.

THE BASICS OF FRICTION AND DIRECTION

Creating friction and direction at the same time is always a challenge. The reason why you should balance friction and direction is simple: Active brains drive engagement, which is needed to increase participation.

This principle will help you to find the perfect balance between how much direction (or guidance) your learners need and how much friction they can handle before you lose them (see Figure 11.1).

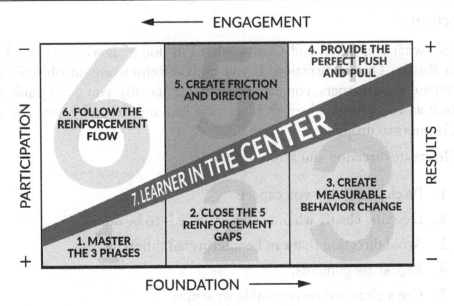

Figure 11.1. Create Friction and Direction

Friction

I define friction as "a situation when the brain needs to work because the presented situation and/or question is not clear." Friction has nothing to do with resistance to your reinforcement program. Just as my coach created friction in my brain by including the Dutch guy I didn't like on our trip to Russia, you need to do something to get your learners' brains fully alert.

To create friction and activate learners' brains, you should:

1. Avoid predictability.
2. Omit some information.
3. Switch the usual order of information.
4. Leave some details to the imagination.
5. Stimulate discussion.
6. Use the "less is more" approach.
7. Write so your words personally touch the learner.
8. Make your messages easy to read.
9. Avoid verbs that don't convey action.

Later in this chapter, I explain how you can create friction in your reinforcement program.

Direction

"I know what you think, and I know what I'm doing" is what my coach told me in Russia. That is direction. If you use the reinforcement objectives and understand your learners, you can guide them. Actually, you don't guide them as much as you prevent them from getting lost and dropping out. You don't want learners to drop out.

To create direction and avoid dropout:

1. Be clear on what you expect.
2. Describe clearly when something needs to be done.
3. Avoid direction that can be interpreted different ways.
4. Repeat assignments.
5. Use a clear and recognizable structure.
6. Give a summary at crucial moments.
7. Encourage the learner to reflect and look to the future.
8. Use questions to check if the learner is on track.
9. Avoid dense text.

Later in this chapter, I explain how to put direction to work in your reinforcement program.

BALANCING FRICTION AND DIRECTION

It is not easy to combine the techniques to create friction with the techniques to create direction. You should know what happens with your learners if you create a program with too little or too much friction in combination with too little or too much direction. In Figure 11.2, you see the effect of different combinations of friction and direction.

Here is a breakdown of each of these combinations:

Low direction, low friction: If you create a program with little direction in combination with low friction, your learners will not be challenged and may not know what they need to do to change their behavior or when they need to do it. The learners will show disinterest, and the consequence is resignation. Even a highly motivated learner will drop off in this situation.

Low direction, high friction: If you keep the direction low but increase the friction, the learners will become confused. The learners' brains

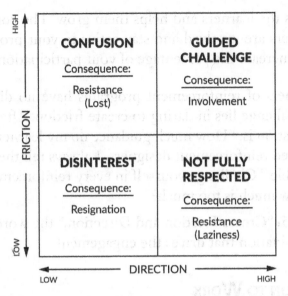

Figure 11.2. Different Combinations of Friction and Direction Result in Different Outcomes

work very hard, but don't have a frame of reference. The consequence is that the learners show resistance because they don't know why you are asking them to change their behavior and what they need to do to change it. They become lost and drop out. This happens with highly motivated learners as well as with not-so-motivated learners. I've seen situations in which designers have to work with less motivated learners. They design a reinforcement program to drive their engagement with lots of friction to challenge the learners and activate their brains. However, in most cases, they achieve exactly the opposite.

High direction, low friction: If you use less friction and increase the direction in your reinforcement program, the learners get only directions without challenging their brains. You treat them as small children. The learners start enthusiastically, but over time they don't feel respected. The consequence is that the learners show resistance because they are not being challenged and their brains are in a state of laziness. This does not motivate the learners to continue your program, so they drop out, and your participation rate decreases.

High direction, high friction: Once you balance the friction and direction at a high level, you start to create what I call "guided challenge." The learners do not understand what's going on, and the challenge creates an alertness, which leads to friction. The direction gives the learners a frame of reference. This combination of friction and direction motivates the learners and helps them grow. The consequence is that the learners are involved and stay active in your program. And active learners increase the percentage of your participation.

Many designers of reinforcement programs have no difficulty in giving direction. The challenge lies in daring to create friction. After you create friction, the next question is: "How much guidance do my learners need?" When I teach inexperienced reinforcement designers, I always tell them, "Give as little direction as possible." Challenge yourself in every reinforcement program and ask yourself, "How much is too much?"

In Principle 5, "Create Friction and Direction," the word "and" is important. It's the combination that drives the engagement.

PUTTING FRICTION TO WORK

To create friction, you must activate learners' brains. But it's difficult to engage brains and keep them active. When you add friction to direction, you keep your learners' brains alert. They think: What's new? How do I solve this challenge? How does this new information fit into all the information I already have? What do I need to do? And so on. The learners' brains need to work.

Timing and patterns

To avoid predictability, simply send your reinforcement messages at different times. If all of your reinforcement messages are sent at 9 a.m. on the same day of the week, your learners will not be curious.

Don't patterns in your series of messages. I often see messages that start with an assignment, then ask for a reflection, and finish with a task to address improvement. It's a common pattern. Why not switch the order? If you want to give an assignment, start with the question to determine specific improvement points. A learner's brain will ask, "Why do I have to do this?" and "Is it logical to answer this question right now?" This occurs in the brain before the person even considers an answer to the question. Use this form of friction to keep learners' brains alert.

Imagination

If you work with scenarios, you can use the learners' imagination to create friction. Have you ever read a book and then seen the movie? Nine out of 10 people will tell you that the movie was not as good as the book. Why? When we read a book, our brains create detailed pictures of the characters and setting. Our brains are actively involved in creating the whole story. While we are watching the movie, we just look at the place the director has created and watch the main characters as they are portrayed by actors.

How do you find the right balance between direction and friction in these scenarios? Focus on direction, just enough so your learners don't get lost in the content. Less is more. Leave something to the imagination. You don't have to be the Steven Spielberg of reinforcement programs.

Social friction

In your reinforcement program, you can also stimulate social friction. If your learners talk with other learners about the ways they applied new knowledge and skills, it will affect their own performance. Discussing and sharing experiences, forces the brain to recall and analyze its experiences. This naturally increases engagement.

Message content

If you take a closer look at the text you use in your messages, you may notice that much of your message has little to no effect on the learners. Their brains are not triggered at all. Common mistakes in messages that kill brain activity include using wording like the following:

- This is important because... (You don't have to explain why it's important.)

- Go to page 24 of your workbook to see an image of . . . (Better to say, "In your workbook, you will find a great image of . . . .)

- As in your last assignment, use your action plan to complete your improvements. (Avoid words like "same" and "last time.")

The words you use in your reinforcement messages are crucial. Most training materials are written in the third person (he, she, it). When you write reinforcement messages, always use the second person (you). This creates a stronger connection to the learners and, therefore, much more impact. Table 11.1 shows you some examples.

Write in the second person (you).

Table 11.1.   Second-Person vs. Third-Person Wording

Second Person	Third Person
Your client	The client
You	The leader or the . . .
Your market	The market
In your role	At company X

PUTTING DIRECTION TO WORK

To create direction, you also need to activate the learners' brains. There is a fine line between friction and direction. When you provide direction, you avoid losing learners because they don't understand the bigger picture and the purpose. With the right direction, learners can see the bigger picture and understand your program's structure.

Keep in mind that their brains need to work, too. If you provide too much direction, you create lazy brains.

Refer to the objectives

When you give an assignment, or create a learning moment, try to integrate the behavior you want to see. This behavior is the bigger picture, your goals for this reinforcement program. For example, "Asking open-ended questions should be second nature during all your sales meetings. During the next three meetings, focus on XYZ." Don't miss this opportunity, and ask the learners to focus on XYZ only during the next three meetings.

Share timing

As designer of the reinforcement program, you know exactly when the learners have a busy week or if a week is less intense. To give direction means also helping the learners know what they can expect. You can tailor your messages before a busy week: "Next week will be a power week. Make sure you plan enough time to prepare your learning moments."

Structure explanation

Give the learners summaries at certain times, like: "During the last two weeks you worked hard to apply your questioning skills. In the next two weeks you will receive assignments on your questioning skills." Don't go into too much detail, but mention the bigger picture. Providing too much detail makes your learners' brains lazy.

A common pitfall in the structure explanation is to explain *why* your learners have to do, to learn, to answer, or to evaluate. Explaining the "why" is not giving direction; it's proving your accountability, not theirs.

PRINCIPLE 5. ASSESSMENT

Consider how you have used Principle 5, "Create Friction and Direction," to keep your learners' brains active. Have you challenged the learners to think about what's new, how they solve this challenge, or how the new information fits with what they already know? Read each statement below and give yourself points based on the following scale:

Poor: 1 point

Fair: 2 points

Good: 3 points

Excellent: 4 points

Principle 5: Create Friction and Direction

The reinforcement program is not predictable.	
Perfect balance exists between friction and direction.	
Just enough direction is provided so the learners avoid getting lost in the content.	
The series of messages uses different patterns.	
The reinforcement program is written in the second person.	
The messages keep their brains alert.	
Social friction is stimulated.	
Communication messages are balanced between specific and general.	
Total Score:	

(You can find a copy of this assessment in the Appendix to this book.)

(continued)

(*continued*)

    If your total score is:

        Less than 17 points: Needs improvement

        17 to 26 points: Needs attention

        27 to 32 points: Good to go

    If your program needs improvement or requires attention, review the nine actions that create direction and then review the nine actions that create friction. Consider how you can work more of these into your reinforcement program.

CHAPTER 12

Principle 6: Follow the Reinforcement Flow

Principle 6 is the third principle to drive your engagement. Principle 4, "Provide the Perfect Push and Pull," helps you increase the involvement of your learners. Principle 5, "Create Friction and Direction," helps you to activate your learners' brains. Principle 6, "Follow the Reinforcement Flow," helps you keep the learners in their grow status (see Figure 12.1).

When you follow the reinforcement flow, all your questions, assignments, and learning objectives are in perfect balance with the skills and knowledge levels of your learners. If your learners develop their skills and knowledge levels, your challenges must become more complex to avoid boredom. Or start with a less complex reinforcement program in the beginning, because if your challenges are too difficult in the beginning, learners will feel anxiety. Within the reinforcement flow, your challenges and skills/knowledge are constantly in balance.

Principles 4 and 5 are meant to keep the learners' brains alert and let them think. Principle 6 is meant to keep the structure and correct level in your reinforcement program. Let's learn how to avoid boredom or anxiety.

THE VALUE OF FEEDBACK

If you want to drive engagement, feedback is crucial. In top-level sports, athletes love to receive feedback. No matter whether it is positive or negative feedback, top athletes are willing to learn. My coach spent lots of time creating the best training program, selecting the best tournaments, developing the perfect team and staff members, and organizing well-structured feedback during my preparation for the Olympics. In practice, feedback is often forgotten or receives too little attention during the reinforcement process, but feedback is needed for growth.

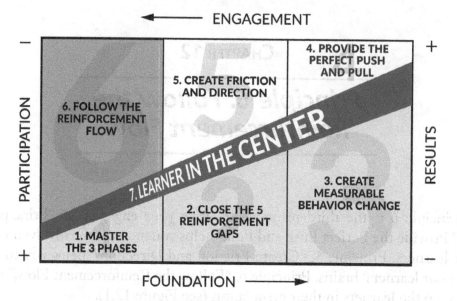

Figure 12.1. Follow the Reinforcement Flow

In your reinforcement program strive to process all four levels of feedback:

1. **Task:** Feedback about a task or an assignment identifies errors and depth of quality and is usually measured against a set of criteria. This feedback can be used to correct misconceptions. You want to know how well the task has been performed—correctly or incorrectly.

2. **Process:** The next level is the process level, which focuses on how the task or assignment was processed. You want to know how the learners approached the assignment. What is the relationship between how they approached the assignment and the quality of their performance? Your learners should give feedback on the strategies they needed to perform the assignment.

3. **Self-Regulation:** The third level of feedback is based on self-regulation. Are your learners able to monitor and control their own learning and growth? Your learners should identify what activities need to be undertaken next to make better progress.

4. **Self:** The self level is about personal evaluation and the effect of behavior change. I recommend using a third person for feedback on the self level. It is a good way to identify blind spots.

THE CCAF MODEL

How can you create valuable feedback in your reinforcement program? The Context, Challenge, Activity, and Feedback (CCAF) Model is great to use in your reinforcement programs.

- *Context* provides a meaningful framework and conditions.
- *Challenge* is a stimulus or urgency to act.
- *Activity* is a response to the challenge.
- *Feedback* is a reflection about the effectiveness of the actions.

Give your learners the opportunity to solve problems that they may encounter at work. It's the first C of the CCAF model, Context. Force learners to make risk-free work-related decisions. Use branching what-if scenarios and case studies, to show learners the consequences of their choices.

In the second C (for Challenge) you recognize Principle 5, "Create Friction and Direction." Don't make the challenge too easy for the learners. Use "distractors," the common misconceptions or easily confused alternative options, to challenge your learners to consider other factors before making their final decisions. Or give them stimuli to search for additional information they need.

The A for Activity determines the quality of your feedback. Your activity in your reinforcement program should neither be too easy nor too difficult for your learners to complete. Being too easy may lead to your learners underestimating the importance of it and becoming bored. If it's too difficult, it may lead them to give up and quit. Effective reinforcement programs balance the levels of difficulty to guarantee engagement. Principle 6, "Follow the Reinforcement Flow," is crucial to obtaining the feedback needed for behavioral change.

EXAMINING FLOW

Before you start using the CCAF Model, let's take a closer look at the definition of flow proposed by psychologist Mihaly Csikszentmihalyi. He said, "With flow comes joy and involvement with life, as well as balance between challenge and the ability to meet the challenge."

How can you use Csikszentmihalyi's definition in your reinforcement programs? How can you create "joy and involvement"? These two key elements drive learner engagement. How can you use "challenge and the ability to meet the challenge"? More precisely, how can you use the balance between the challenge and the ability to meet the challenge. It's all about the balance, the perfect fit.

> *Reinforcement flow is all about balancing skills and challenges.*

Kees became Dutch lightweight champion in 's-Hertogenbosch, Holland, on November 3, 1991. After a day of competition, he was in the final. Kees seemed to be in control the whole day. I was very nervous, more nervous than for my own matches. He started very strong, full of self-confidence. Halfway through the final, they came into the ground fight, called Newaza in Japanese. I had never seen Kees be so quick. He attacked with a strangulation and his opponent tapped the mat three times, signaling "I give up." Kees' unique strangulation technique was later known as the "Kees Choke." Later, Kees told me that he had never used this technique in competition and kept it as a surprise attack, which worked. I was so proud that my brother was national champion.

After he received his gold medal and the national anthem had played, he was interviewed by a reporter from the national television station. The reporter asked, "You started this morning and already seemed the champion. What makes you the champion today?" Kees answered, "Because I was in my flow." He paused and then repeated, "Yes, it was because I was in a flow."

The pause made Kees' statement very powerful. After that weekend, Kees and I talked about that interview and his flow statement. As athletes, we like to understand the flow situation. Everything felt perfect, everything was in balance, everything was a perfect fit. What could we do to create flow for every tournament? You hear about the flow situation a lot when champions are interviewed. I bet you will recognize this feeling from now on.

Balancing skills and challenges

What exactly is the flow and how can you use it in your reinforcement program to drive engagement? Flow is the balance between the current skills and challenges.

Look at Figure 12.2. If the assignment or the challenge is too easy compared with the skill level of your learners, your learners become bored and frustrated. If the assignment or challenge is too difficult compared with the skill level of your learners, your learners become anxious and frustrated. Neither situation is good for engagement in your reinforcement program; they mean lower participation by your learners.

Using Principle 6 means finding that balance between challenges and skills. In a good reinforcement program, skills develop over time. How do the challenges or assignments match this development? Are you using more difficult scenarios, more difficult questions, over time or are you asking questions for which a tiny detail is the difference between correct and incorrect?

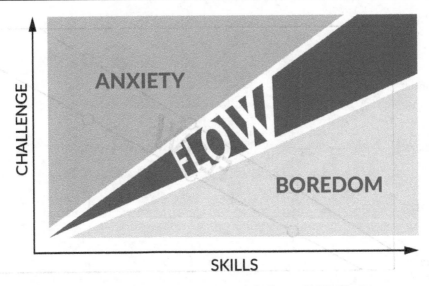

Figure 12.2.   Flow Is the Balance Between Skills and Challenges

Check your assignments and challenges in your reinforcement program and compare them with the expected skills level of the learners. Is your reinforcement program following the reinforcement flow?

If your score ends up in the *boredom* section, you need to increase the difficulty of the assignments or challenges. Also check Principle 5, "Create Friction and Direction," to ensure you don't create lazy brains. Check the questions or answers and make sure they become more difficult over time. If your score is in the *anxiety* section, decrease the difficulty, especially at the beginning of your program. The pitfall is that you might decide to spell out every detail. That is not decreasing the difficulty. Make the differences between the answers clearer or reduce the complexity of the assignments.

If you use the perfect reinforcement flow, you balance the challenges and the skills development, as shown in Figure 12.3. Keep in mind that this drives your learners' engagement.

When I look back at my Judo career, it's clear that over the years each tournament becomes more difficult and more challenging. As young talents, Kees and I went to lots of tournaments in and around Holland. In the next phase, we went to European cup matches. As we grew more skilled, the tournaments became more prestigious, the opponents stronger, the different Judo styles from all over the world more complex, and winning a medal more difficult. Our trainer always looked for the best fit between our newly developed skills and tournament level. In other words, he found the flow to keep us motivated and engaged to train five or six hours every day. In sports it's a normal process. How is the flow of your reinforcement program?

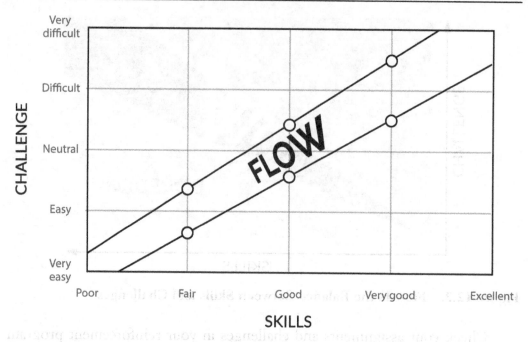

SKILLS

Figure 12.3.   Balancing Challenges and Skills Development

Table 12.1 shows the three most common pitfalls to creating your reinforcement flow.

Table 12.1.   Three Common Pitfalls and Solutions for Reinforcement Flow

Pitfall	Solution
No back and forth move between challenge and reward	If the challenge requires critical thinking and is mildly challenging for the learner, it can be satisfying. The learner can feel rewarded by meeting the challenge and motivated to keep learning. The ideal reinforcement flow moves back and forth between challenging and rewarding your learners.
No break for the learner	When planning your reinforcement flow, remember to give learners a break. If you do not give learners a chance to "rest" or time to work on their skills during reinforcement, they will become frustrated and take their own "breaks." That means a dropout and low participation as a result.
No feedback to guide behavior change	Promote engagement by rewarding accomplishments and use frequent, multifaceted feedback to guide behavior. Use all four levels of feedback.

Going against the flow

Although Csikszentmihalyi's definition says that flow stimulates joy and involvement, also not following the flow can lead to a higher commitment and involvement.

Forced out of the comfort zone

In the summer of 1989, the Dutch Judo Federation invited me to compete at the World Championships for seniors in Belgrade. I was just over 20 years old and still a junior competitor. I was so proud because this was the highest level of competition, beside the Olympic Games, of course.

After we flew to Belgrade, I got my accreditation as an official fighter for Holland, passed the first weight control, and received the fighting schedule. My first fight was against a strong guy from Eastern Europe. The guy had muscles everywhere, a beard and—compared with my junior body—was a real killer. I didn't sleep at all that night.

The next morning, as we drove from the hotel to the arena, I did not say a word. But my brain was working very hard and was full of thoughts. The pride of being selected for the World Championship changed into fear and anxiety. This challenge was too difficult. I started to doubt myself. I was absolutely not in my flow.

The fight against the Eastern European athlete lasted 14 seconds, including the time it took for me to stand up after he threw me on the ground. Fourteen seconds! This challenge was apparently not in balance with my skills. Not yet.

At the end of the day, my coach and I evaluated my performance. I asked, "Why did you let me fight at the World Championship?"

"This is what you needed to grow," my coach answered.

I realized that my performance during this tournament was a hard wake-up call, giving me a chance to measure myself against the highest level of Judo. I knew what I had to do during the next three years to advance toward the Olympic Games; I had to work very hard and close the skills gap.

My coach continued, "To grow, you have to leave your comfort zone." He forced me into my panic zone intentionally. The challenge of this World Championship was way too difficult compared with my skills level at that time. Once I realized that, I was motivated to work hard on my skill-set.

As I developed my skill-set, the challenges my coach gave me became harder. But since Belgrade, the challenges were always in balance with my skills level. We stay in the flow. My coach took a risk to force me into the panic zone in Belgrade, but when it turned out well.

The same happened with my comfort zone, that zone where you feel safe and comfortable. When you're in your comfort zone, the fear of new challenges limits the new actions and initiatives. My coach never let me stay long in the comfort zone. Once I felt a little bit comfortable, he gave me a new challenge.

Facing the panic zone

The first time I went to Japan, I was 18 years old. After a long travel day and a good night of rest, I was ready to go to the training. My first training was with 240 Japanese fighters at Tokai University in Tokyo. I was excited, ready for action, and confident.

When I entered the dojo (practice area) I moved from my flow zone into my panic zone. Two hundred and forty Japanese fighters, all with shaved heads, looked at me, and I felt as if they were all silently saying, "So you think you're going to survive here?" Their joint answer was easy to guess: "No."

Balancing between my panic zone and my flow zone, I started the training. In the beginning, I spent a lot of time in my panic zone, but after some weeks I started to get more comfortable and my fear disappeared. I enjoyed the hard training and was not impressed anymore by all the shaved Japanese fighters. I even shaved my head.

My new life in Japan eventually became routine. I knew the way to the dojo, I recognized the smell of incense from the temple, I ate at my favorite restaurants that served Jiaozi, a kind of dumpling, and I became friends with some Japanese Judo fighters. I moved from panic zone through the flow zone into my comfort zone. "Tokai University is great. I can live here forever," I thought one day.

That day, my coach told me that we were moving to the University of Tsukuba, a notorious university known for Spartan trainings methods. My comfort zone was gone. Flow zone or panic zone?

I went through the same process as I had in Tokyo. First, I experienced the panic zone, but not as intensely as in Tokyo, and soon I was in my flow zone. I realized that I was developing myself, and my comfort zone became bigger. And because of that, my coach kept creating bigger challenges to keep me in my flow zone. As an Olympic athlete, I lived continuously in the flow zone.

USING REINFORCEMENT FLOW TO GROW

When you use the reinforcement flow to leave the comfort zone, your focus is on growth. As you know, your learners enjoy the security and predictability of their daily routines. They fear rejection, judgment, and failure. They avoid risk and the unknown. Think about the Prospect Theory (refer to Chapter 2). A comfort zone relates to anxiety levels. It is defined in psychology as an artificial mental boundary; a place or situation in which your learner feels safe, comfortable, in control, or at ease and without stress. The comfort zone allows for a predictable routine to minimize stress.

Use the Reinforcement Flow to leave the comfort zone.

It's easy to be comfortable, and there's nothing wrong with having somewhere familiar to return to. But too much comfort can make your learners lazy and kill productivity and performance (see Figure 12.4). It's hard for your learners to motivate themselves to make real improvements while feeling content. Your learners will do just enough to get by. This will lead to missed opportunities and regret.

It will take your learners a lot of courage to break out of their comfort zones, but keep in mind it can be great for their self-esteem, motivation, and lasting happiness and fulfillment. In other words, engagement. Learning to face the unknown not only becomes easier with practice, but can be very liberating and surprisingly behavior forming. After my first trip to Japan, many other trips to this Judo Mecca followed.

If you want to use your reinforcement program to help your learners to leave their comfort zones, don't "push" them too far. Stay within the learning

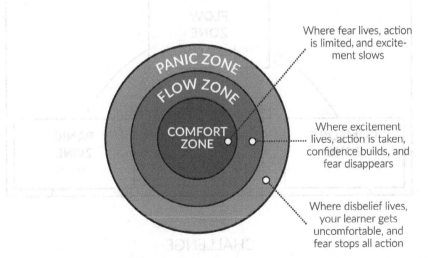

Figure 12.4. Push Your Learners from Their Comfort Zones to Their Flow Zones

zone or, as I call it, the flow zone. This zone includes excitement, actions, feedback, learning, and development. In the flow zone, confidence is built, and fear disappears.

If you push learners too far, or if your challenges are too complex or way too difficult compared with their current skill-sets, learners may end up in the panic zone. In this zone, learners feel very uncomfortable and may completely block and all actions and initiatives because of fear. This zone kills productivity and performance.

To drive engagement and increase the percentage of participation, your learners need challenges and success. Success can be seen as good performance, based on the determined reinforcement objective. Learners in the flow zone can deliver peak performance and show the desired change in behavior.

The performance curve in Figure 12.5 shows that, in both the comfort zone and the panic zone, performance is low. If you increase the challenge, the learners will move into the flow zone and achieve an increase in performance. Don't challenge them too much because if they fall into the panic zone, their performance will drop. You must balance the skills and the challenges to create peak performance.

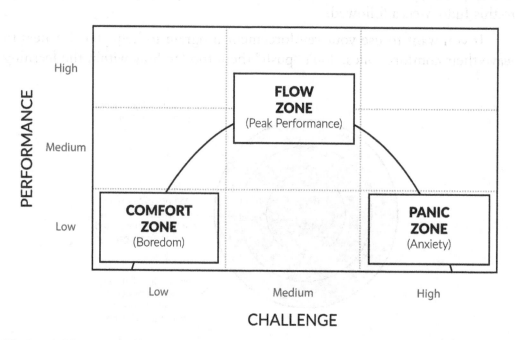

Figure 12.5.   A Challenge Moves Learners into the Flow Zone and Results in a
            Performance Increase

PRINCIPLE 6. ASSESSMENT

How did you create the reinforcement flow to balance your learners' skills with the challenges you gave them? How do you motivate the learners to leave their comfort zones? Read each statement below and give yourself points based on the following scale:

Poor: 1 point

Fair: 2 points

Good: 3 points

Excellent: 4 points

Principle 6: Follow the Reinforcement Flow

The program offers perfect flow, balanced between challenges and skills.	
More difficult questions (not answers) are used over time.	
Details in the answers distinguish between correct and incorrect responses.	
Some challenges are out of the learners' comfort zones.	
Skills will develop over time, so the challenges in the scenarios do also.	
The learners feel rewarded by meeting each challenge.	
The CCAF Model is followed.	
A variety of feedback mechanisms keeps learners informed.	
The program moves back and forth between challenging and rewarding learners.	
Learners can see the next goal in order to progress.	
Learners can "rest" or have time to work on their skills.	
Total Score:	

(You can find a copy of this assessment in the Appendix to this book.)

If your total score is:

Less than 22 points: Needs improvement

22 to 35 points: Needs attention

36 to 44 points: Good to go

(continued)

(continued)

If your program needs improvement or attention, check how you organized the feedback and how that helps learners to move into the flow zone. Double-check the flow assessment and see whether your challenges are too difficult or too easy. Are they becoming more difficult over time?

CHAPTER 13

Recap of Engagement

U p to this point, you have created a strong foundation with Principles 1, 2, and 3, and are driving the engagement with Principles 4, 5, and 6.

Let's recap the three principles that help you drive engagement. A focus on engagement is needed to increase participation. Read this recap carefully and be sure you have no more questions before moving to Principle 7, "Place the Learner in the Center."

PRINCIPLE 4: PROVIDE THE PERFECT PUSH AND PULL

1. The brain sucks up 20 percent of your overall energy. Your brain is always looking for shortcuts that will allow it to avoid using energy. For that reason, you continually need to "push" the brain and avoid using shortcuts, or else stop mastering new knowledge and skills.

2. Not all your push is a pull.

3. A perfect balance between 40 and 65 percent is pull.

4. Check your reinforcement program, and use the pull thermometer in Figure 10.2. If your score is below 35 percent, your program has characteristics of a micro learning module.

5. If your score is above 70 percent, you have a lot of pull messages. Too many and your program has characteristics of an assessment.

6. Use memory techniques to update knowledge and avoid mistakes.

PRINCIPLE 5: CREATE FRICTION AND DIRECTION

- Friction is when brains need to work because the situation and/or question presented is not clear or completely spelled out.

- To create friction and activate learners' brains, you should:
  1. Avoid predictability.
  2. Omit some information.
  3. Switch the usual order of information.
  4. Leave some details to the imagination.
  5. Stimulate discussion.
  6. Use the "less is more" approach.
  7. Write so your words personally touch the learner.
  8. Make your messages easy to read.
  9. Avoid verbs that don't convey action.
- To create direction and avoid learners dropping out, you should:
  1. Be clear on what you expect.
  2. Describe clearly what needs to be done.
  3. Avoid giving direction that can be interpreted different ways.
  4. Repeat assignments.
  5. Use a clear and recognizable structure.
  6. Summarize at crucial moments.
  7. Encourage learners to reflect and look to the future.
  8. Use questions to check whether learners are on track.
  9. Avoid dense text.
- Balance between low and high direction and low and high friction. High direction and high friction results in a "guided challenge."
- How much is too much?
- Write in the second person, avoiding the third person.

Second Person	Third Person
Your client	The client
You	The leader or the . . .
Your market	The market
In your role	At company X

- All messages keep the brains in an alert mode and don't kill brain activity.
- Stimulate social friction.

PRINCIPLE 6: FOLLOW THE REINFORCEMENT FLOW

- In your reinforcement program, strive to process all four levels of feedback:
  - Task.
  - Process.
  - Self-Regulation.
  - Self.
- The CCAF model is a great to use in your reinforcement program.
- Reinforcement flow is all about balancing skills and challenges.
- Check your reinforcement flow.
- Use more difficult questions (not the answers) over time.
- Three common pitfalls exist while creating your reinforcement flow:
  - *No* back and forth move between challenge and rewarding.
  - *No* break for the learner.
  - *No* feedback to guide behavior change.
- Use the three zones: comfort, flow, and panic.
- If you want to use your reinforcement program to help your learners to leave their comfort zones, don't "push" them too far. Stay within the flow zone.
- To grow, you should leave your comfort zone. The reinforcement flow helps learners leave the comfort zone.
- Check the performance curve for peak performance.

CHAPTER 14

Principle 7: Place the Learner in the Center

This seems like an obvious principle, but I often see it as the missing link in reinforcement programs. Principle 7 is the connection between *foundation* and *engagement*.

If you compare the three principles you used for building your foundation with the three principles to create engagement you will recognize that:

1. Building the foundation starts with the perfect balance of the 3 phases (Principle 1); creating engagement starts with a balance between push and pull (Principle 4).

2. Closing the 5 gaps (Principle 2) is required to have a solid foundation; friction and direction (Principle 5) are required to let the learners' brains work hard and drives involvement.

3. To create measurable behavior change (Principle 3) requires that you use your measurement plan and verify the performance; by following the reinforcement flow (Principle 6), you optimize the peak performance of the learners.

Reinforcement is like an Olympic program. The focus is on balance, conditions, and performance.

> *Design of reinforcement focuses on balance, conditions, and performance.*

PROJECT WURTH

My coach started his design of my Olympic program as soon as the Olympic Games in Seoul finished in 1988. He was responsible for my achieving a good result four years later. His responsibility was to create a well-thought-out program that led to success and prevented me from dropping out early. He focused on three important elements: balance, conditions, and performance.

He created balance in the program by guiding me in my behavior change, step by step. He started by asking: "Is it your choice to become an Olympic champion?" My answer was the start of a great journey. I changed my behavior so that I slowly became more and more an Olympic athlete. My family, my friends, my studies, my social network, my life, all changed because I said yes to a dream.

This was a carefully built process guided by my coach and balanced with my personal development. He knew what was needed, but *I* determined the tempo. If my personal development was not quick enough, he pushed me forward or pulled me back and evaluated my progress. Everything was based on steady growth.

He also created good conditions. Over time we closed all gaps needed to perform at an Olympic level. My knowledge went up, and my coach made sure that I avoided conditions that would have been demotivating. He created many ways for me to practice new skills. When I was down or depressed or broken because of disappointing results, or when I thought my progress was too slow, he created new ways to motivate me. He made me think and created friction, but I never got lost.

And, of course, everything was measured. My staff of more than 15 people knew everything about me. I was an open book. My weight trainer, condition trainer, video analyst, doctor, coach, manager, dietitian, technical trainer, mental trainer, physiotherapist—they all knew the state of my body and mental health. They worked for four years on "Project Wurth." Based on all this knowledge and the outcome of these measurements, these professionals decided how Project Wurth could leave his comfort zone and get into the flow to create peak performance.

What was the most important part of this Olympic program? The balance, the conditions, or the performance? Before I give you the answer, I want to emphasize that these three elements are crucial to gain results and drive participation. But the most important part was me. I was in the center of this Olympic journey. Everybody, the whole staff, and everything that was created, thought of, measured, evaluated, or changed was part of that one goal: *me* becoming an Olympic champion. There was no guarantee that we would achieve this goal, but we all knew that if I was not in the center, we certainly would not make it. Principle 7, "Place the Learner in the Center," will help you place your learners centrally.

FOCUS ON THE LEARNER

Principle 7 relates to all other principles (see Figure 14.1). No matter whether you build a strong foundation to gain results or drive the engagement to increase your percentage of participation, always place the learner in the center.

To be sure you have used Principle 7 throughout your reinforcement program, review this checklist. Answer yes to each of the six statements that is true of your program. Be very critical. You can think about it easily; your learners won't.

The learner is in the center of the reinforcement program because:

- The learners are more important than the content.
- The program continually adds value for the learners.
- The focus is on the minimum a learner need to know or to do at each moment.
- The program is not retraining but helping the learners to apply knowledge and skills.
- The foundation is so strong that the learners are changing behavior and creating impact in the organization.
- The engagement is fully based on the learners' experiences and drives 100 percent participation.

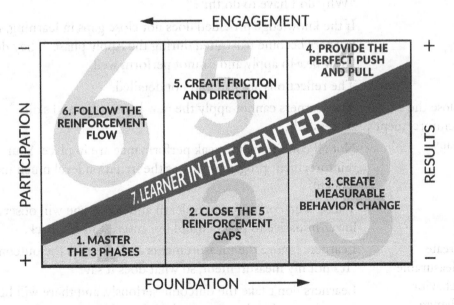

Figure 14.1. Put the Learner in the Center

Think and act like a top athlete; always looking for feedback. Ask your colleagues to review your program and let them focus on Principle 7. Is the learner in the center?

Would I complete my own reinforcement program?

If you apply Principle 7 and build your foundation and drive the engagement based on the other six principles, your reinforcement will succeed. But what happens if your learners are not in the center? What behavior might you perceive? What will be the result of your reinforcement program? If the learner is not in the center, it's hard to realize lasting results and even harder to keep the learners motivated and avoid dropout.

If learners are not in the center, each principle has its own indicators of this, as listed in Table 14.1.

Table 14.1.   Placing Learners in the Center of Each Principle

Principle	If Learners Are NOT in the Center
1. Master the 3 Phases for Results	Learners do not recognize the phases of your program and start raising questions at the wrong times.
	The *Why* question is not based on awareness, but on frustration: "Why do I have to do this?"
	If the knowledge provided does not close gaps in learning, the learners become frustrated during the Apply phase. They don't know *how* to apply and cannot perform well.
	The reflections are bad and not detailed.
2. Close the 5 Reinforcement Gaps	The learners cannot apply the new knowledge and skills successfully.
	Not all conditions for peak performance are in place. Your reinforcement program reaches the irritation level much more quickly.
	There is no commitment to learn and grow; you will observe lower initiative to practice and less interest in feedback.
3. Create Measurable Behavior Change	Learners ignore the measurements and question the outcome: "It's not my measurement, so what does it say?"
	Learners don't take the outcome seriously, and there will be less commitment for the program based on the measurements.

Principle	If Learners Are NOT in the Center
4. Provide the Perfect Push and Pull	Learners do not recognize the push and pull messages as helpful to their personal development. The behavior you will observe is based on shortcuts and laziness.
	Learner will raise questions like "Why should I go for the max? It's not for me."
	You will observe more mistakes because the learners cannot remember the content or recognize the push and pull communication messages: "It's not clear to me."
5. Create Friction and Direction	Learners don't recognize themselves in the third person communication style. It's too general: "That's not me."
	Learners use the friction as an excuse instead of a challenge and inspiration for their brains.
6. Follow the Reinforcement Flow	Learners show no excitement. They resist new challenges. They don't believe in the added value for them.
	Learners stay in their comfort zones and use the unknown and fear as an excuse not to move. And even when they move out of their comfort zones, you will see that the commitment is not 100 percent.

THE LEARNERS' INTENTION

The behavior change you want to achieve with your reinforcement program must align with the learners' intention to perform certain behaviors. Generally, the stronger the intention, the more likely the behavior will be performed. Principle 7 is meant to drive learners' intention. According to the Theory of Planned Behavior (Ajzen, 1988), three determinants explain behavioral intention:

1. The attitude (the learners' opinion about the new behavior).

2. The subjective norm (opinions of others about the behavior learners need to perform).

3. The perceived behavioral control (the learners' perception of the extent to which performance of the behavior is easy or difficult).

If you focus on the attitude, subjective norm, and the perceived behavioral control, you influence the intention. And the intention is the learners' motivation to perform certain behavior. Principle 7, "Place the Learner in the Center," guides you to focus on the learners' intention.

Once your reinforcement program is being used by your learners, you can observe their intentions and their motivation. If the learners are in the center, you will observe that learners are:

1. Consciously engaged in asking for and applying feedback.

2. Looking for additional knowledge.

3. Curious about results and progress.

4. Not falling behind with applying your reinforcement messages and following your program structure.

5. Attentive in discussions about the reinforcement topic and proactively looking for "social friction."

6. Exceeding your expectations and looking for challenges outside their comfort zones.

7. Taking time to apply, appreciate, and measure results.

Although I was super-motivated as an athlete and my intention was to become an Olympic champion, my coach always observed my actions. Did I use lots of excuses? Did I avoid taking risks? Or was I grumpy? He looked at the way I walked, how I talked with others, how I came to the dojo, what questions I had. Everything was important to him. He knew his training program and staff were perfectly built around Project Wurth, but even then, he observed me all the time. He always knew when something was wrong.

I remember a specific example. It was a Wednesday afternoon, three days before a fight. I had just finished my eight-mile run to sweat and lose weight before this fight. This time I had started to lose weight way too late. I needed to sweat and limit my drinking. Every glass of water counts. This was, of course, not good and very unprofessional. After I came back from my run, I checked my weight, still eight pounds to go. I was so angry and frustrated that I threw my running shoes against my living room wall.

I went to the dojo for Judo training that evening and did not say anything. The training was a nightmare. Nothing worked. My timing was off, I was frustrated, I hurt my hand as I grabbed my training partners, and I blamed them for not being careful and being rude.

My coach came to me and asked, "Anthonie, are you OK?" I start to cry and collapsed from shame. He did not ask for more details. He just said, "No more training until the fight." He changed his schedule and sent me home.

After that weekend, he came to my home and we evaluated my performance. He told me that he had known two weeks earlier that this was going to happen—just by observing. We talked about changes in the program and why this had happened.

Apply the lessons from my story to your learners and your reinforcement program:

- Look at your learners. What do you observe?
- What changes can you make in your reinforcement program?

AN ADAPTIVE APPROACH

An efficient way of using Principle 7 is in an *adaptive* reinforcement program. It's hard to build one reinforcement program for each individual learner, for each department, for each culture, for each.... With an adaptive approach, you can manage your reinforcement programs and use Principle 7.

My coach created the ideal path from the moment in that locker room in 1987 when he asked me whether I chose to become an Olympic champion until Thursday, July 30, 1992, in Barcelona. His path included a solid foundation to achieve results, and then he made sure to drive my engagement and keep me motivated until the end.

Did we succeed in following that path exactly as he planned? No. Based on what happened during those six years, my coach had to adapt my Olympic program. I suffered a serious back injury in 1990 that changed his ideal path considerably. But my development also influenced the program. At different times, I needed more weight training or speed training. At one point, my mental training was more successful than expected. Everything influenced the program. We started with an ideal path, but the adaptive approach created the result.

> *Adaptive reinforcement creates the results.*

Adaptive reinforcement allows you to personalize your program, especially when you give learners partial ownership. They will be encouraged to make responsible choices to complete the program. It drives their engagement because it's their choice.

Basically, there are two types of adaptive reinforcement, on demand and automated. Table 14.2 shows some examples of each. If you want to create an adaptive reinforcement program, combine both approaches in a balanced way.

Table 14.2.   Examples of Adaptive Reinforcement

On Demand (by the Learner)	Automated (by the System)
A learner requests additional knowledge.	If the knowledge level is lower than 75 percent correct, the system redirects the learner to additional content.
Pace of the program or intensity changes.	If the reinforcement relates to an assessment tool that, for example, indicates a learning style, the system automatically provides preferred content.
Select additional assignments to practice.	If an answer on a survey question triggers an action, such as not using a form, or a learner is still not comfortable, the system can send additional tools or information.
Select module to reinforce an objective the learner needs for behavior change.	If the progress and the development are above the set criteria, the system can skip or speed up the reinforcement process.

PART 4

ANALYZING YOUR REINFORCEMENT PROGRAM

After you complete all the principles in the reinforcement program, you need to determine whether it's producing the outcomes you desire. Are the Foundation Principles and Engagement Principles in balance, or is one area stronger than the other?

This section helps you assess the shortcomings and strengths of your reinforcement program. You will also find out how to write strong reinforcement messages that will have an impact on your learners and how to tailor your reinforcement program for different types of training.

CHAPTER 15

Finding Balance with the Reinforcement Lever

My first fight at a tournament was always against the scale. On the day of the tournament, all of the competitors must weigh-in by 6 a.m. In the days leading up to the tournament, I would not eat or drink a lot. I wore a sweatsuit in the sauna to help the sweating process. After the sauna, I wouldn't eat or drink, except for perhaps a small sip of water to avoid my lips drying out. During this time, I was constantly thirsty, had no energy left to train, and would spend the 24 hours before the tournament counting how much time was left until the weigh-in.

The scale is ruthless. One ounce too heavy means disqualification. No fight. Every athlete had to defeat the scale first. The weigh-in at 6 a.m. during my first big tournament was not in my comfort zone. The organization selected a conference room in the hotel as the weigh-in room. When I entered the room, I saw about eighty athletes standing in their underwear, waiting until they could weigh. I joined the end of the line.

It took about two minutes per fighter to check their weight, passport, and accreditations. After two hours, it was finally my turn. My weight was in accordance with my accreditation. I could fight that day.

However, it was already 8 a.m., and the competition started at 10 a.m. My body needed water and some food to rebuild some strength. Two hours was very little time to replenish my system.

After competing in a few tournaments, the weigh-in procedure became familiar, and I knew what to do. It became part of my comfort zone. I figured out that I shouldn't wait in the line and lose two hours of recovery for the tournament. After that, both Kees and I were some of the first to stand on the scale.

That scale only measured our weight in our underwear. It didn't matter whether we trained hard or had followed the ideal path. It was yes or no, even before we could gain results and win medals.

The Reinforcement Lever is more complex. It shows you the balance between your foundation and your engagement. An imbalance will lead to no

143

results. This is your first fight to win gold with your reinforcement program. Are the foundation and the engagement in balance?

An imbalance leads to no results.

UNDERSTANDING REINFORCEMENT LEVERS

The Reinforcement Lever shows you the balance between results and participation. If you want to create impact in your organization, your reinforcement program must focus on both results and participation. Focusing on results without learners will not create any change in your organization. And it's the same the other way around: if you have a lot of learners (high participation score) but no focus on results, your organization will not change. Results and participation go hand in hand. What balance leads to behavior change and impact?

The Foundation and the Engagement Assessments are based on how well you applied all the principles. The Foundation is based on Principles 1, 2, and 3, and the Engagement on principles 4, 5, and 6. The Reinforcement Lever reflects how well you balanced all principles and how well you placed the learners in the center of your reinforcement program, Principle 7.

The angle of inclination influences the shape of the Reinforcement Levers you can have. If you scored the maximum score on both assessments, your Reinforcement Lever has the angle of inclination shown in Figure 15.1.

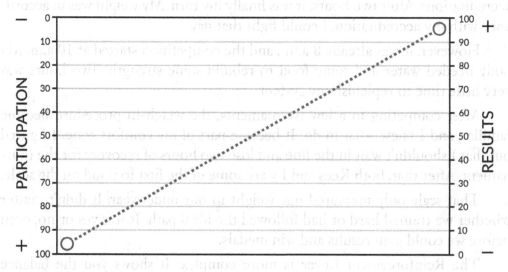

Figure 15.1. A Reinforcement Lever Based on Perfect Foundation and Engagement Assessments

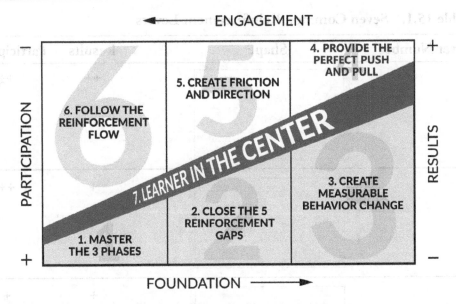

Figure 15.2.   Principles 1 Through 6 Influence Principle 7

When your lever has this angle of inclination, you recognize the importance of Principle 7 in our model, shown in Figure 15.2. In this model, it's clear to see how Principles 1, 2, and 3 influence the angle of inclination. Same for principles 4, 5, and 6.

You want to strive for a 45-degree angle of inclination, starting at the bottom left. If you have a 45-degree angle starting at the top left, you have a big challenge to improve your reinforcement program. Your scores on both assessments are zero.

Next we'll see how to interpret the shape of your reinforcement lever if your angle is less than 45 degrees—or even horizontal. The position of the fulcrum is important to know. Is the fulcrum positioned at the bottom, in the middle, or closer to the top? The ideal position of the fulcrum is exactly in the middle of the scoring overview.

The ideal Reinforcement Lever has a:

- *45-degree angle inclination.*
- *A fulcrum in the middle.*

In Table 15.1 are the most common reinforcement levers, a total of seven shapes.

Table 15.1. Seven Common Reinforcement Levers

Lever Number	Shape	Results	Participation
1		++	++
2		+	++
3		+	+
4		++	–
5		+	–
6		–	++
7		–	–

Many different reinforcement levers are possible, more than I can show here. In the following section, you have the opportunity to chart your scores from the foundation and engagement assessments and see what your own reinforcement lever looks like.

PLOTTING YOUR REINFORCEMENT LEVER

If you completed all of the principle assessments, you have to add up the scores from your Foundation Assessment (Principle 1, 2, and 3) and your Engagement Assessment (Principle 4, 5, and 6). You can use these scores to create your own reinforcement lever.

In Figure 15.3, you can create your reinforcement lever by adding your overall scores from the Foundation and Engagement assessments. Find your score on the bars (Foundation score on Results bar and Engagement score on the Participation bar) and connect the two scores with a straight line and you have your reinforcement lever. It's that easy.

Analyze the shape of your reinforcement lever and consider how you can improve the angle of inclination. The line's angle indicates where there is room for improvement. The maximum score per assessment is 100 points. If you have a perfect score on both assessments, you did a good job. Well done.

Compare your reinforcement lever with the shapes shown in Table 15.1. Check the angle of inclination and the position of the fulcrum. How did you perform?

After you've built your reinforcement program, use your reinforcement lever to see how well you are doing. Ask between two and five other people from your team or other departments to complete these assessments, too. Find the average score to see how the group thinks you're doing overall.

Figure 15.3.   Create Your Own Reinforcement Lever

Good discussions on the angle of inclination will help you determine your development areas. If you have these discussions with your team members, avoid explaining *what* you did and focus on *why* you made certain choices.

> *Focus on the* why *instead of explaining the* what.

ANALYZING THE DIFFERENT REINFORCEMENT LEVERS

In Table 15.1, the different shapes are ranked based on a strong or a weak reinforcement program, numbered from 1 to 7. The shape of reinforcement lever 1 indicates the strongest reinforcement program, focused on great results and good participation. The shape of reinforcement lever 7 indicates a very weak reinforcement program; it will gain no results and no participation. The reinforcement levers are ranked based on results first and participation second. To create behavioral change and impact in your organization, don't focus on one of these outcomes; find the correct balance.

Every lever shape has a reason. In the sections that follow, I will explain each of the seven shapes and encourage you to improve, if the shape represents your lever.

You have completed both the foundation and engagement assessments. By shape of the reinforcement lever, I have made suggestions for improvements. It is important to analyze your score for each principle. To help you quickly see the areas that need improvement, use Table 15.2. Complete the "My Score" column to know where your focus should be when you analyze your reinforcement lever. (These tools are also in the Appendix to this book.)

Table 15.2. Principle Scores Overview

Principle	Max Score	My Score	Attention	Improvement
1. Master the 3 Phases	24	☐	11–16	< 11
2. Close the 5 Reinforcement Gaps	32	☐	14–23	< 14
3. Create Measurable Behavior Change	44	☐	20–32	< 20
4. Provide the Perfect Push and Pull	24	☐	12–19	< 12
5. Create Friction and Direction	32	☐	17–26	< 17
6. Follow the Reinforcement Flow	44	☐	22–35	< 22

Shapes 1 through 3 gain results and drive participation. The improvement for shapes 1 through 3 is less radical. The + and – in Table 15.1 indicate the effect on results and participation. Shapes 1 through 3 fall in the "optimize" category. Shapes 4 through 7 need changes. The – and – indicate little or, in worst-case scenarios, no results or participation. If you have these shapes, you must intervene.

The position of the fulcrum also determines your improvements. If its position is lower than the middle point of the overview, your focus needs to be on the *foundation* (Principles 1, 2, and 3). If the position of the fulcrum is above the middle point, your focus for improvement should be on *engagement* (Principles 4, 5, and 6).

I have a question for you: if the fulcrum is close to the middle point and your reinforcement lever shows an angle of inclination less than 45 degrees, what should you improve?

A Foundation.   **C** Foundation and Engagement.

B Engagement.   **D** Nothing.

The correct answer is C, foundation *and* engagement. Your development focus should be on all six principles. Remember, Behavior Change = Foundation × Engagement, **BC = F × E**. Check your assessment for each principle and improve with small, specific steps. Focus on your development to get the fulcrum in the middle of the overview and at the same time balance improvements on results (1, 2, and 3) and drive participation (4, 5, and 6).

Shape 1

If your reinforcement lever looks like Figure 15.4, congratulations. You applied all 7 Principles well, and your program is ready to launch. Challenge yourself

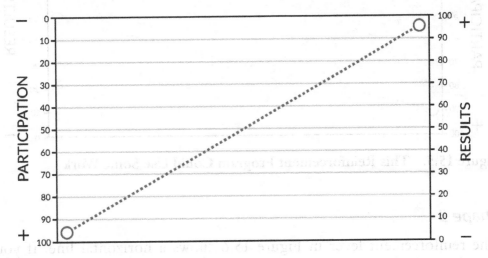

Figure 15.4. A Solid Reinforcement Program

and use the S.A.F.E. method, as described in Chapter 16, to determine how well you wrote your reinforcement messages.

Shape 2

In Figure 15.5, the score of the engagement assessment is high (or high enough), and you have a lower score (between 70 and 40 points) on the foundation assessment. Because of this, the angle of inclination is less than 45 degrees. The same shape comes up if your score on the foundation assessment is high (or high enough), and the score of the engagement assessment is lower, between 40 and 70 points. In both situations, the angle of inclination is less than 45 degrees.

It's important to strive for a 45-degree lever. So, if yours looks like Figure 15.5, you need to improve Principle 1, 2, or 3. If you have the same shape (less than 45 degrees) but your score on the engagement is between 40 and 70, you need to improve Principle 4, 5, or 6. Although the shapes appear to be the same, your improvement areas are totally different.

Check the shapes in sections 3 through 7 to discover how you can improve your score on each topic.

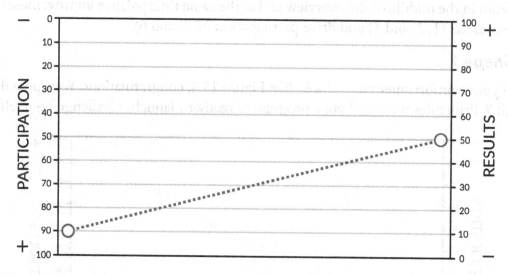

Figure 15.5.   This Reinforcement Program Could Use Some Work

Shape 3

The reinforcement lever in Figure 15.6 shows a horizontal line. If your lever has this shape, your reinforcement program will lead to some results

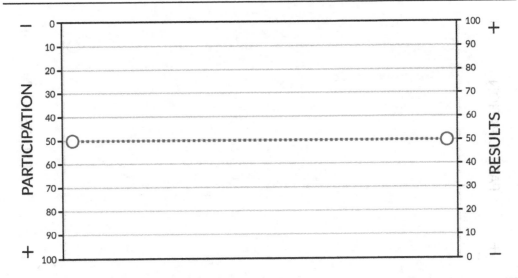

Figure 15.6.   A Mediocre Reinforcement Program

and will drive some participation, but it is a mediocre program. The strong part of this reinforcement program is that this lever has a fulcrum in the middle of the overview. So at least the foundation and engagement principles are in balance.

Two other reinforcement levers are horizontal, but they don't have the fulcrum in the middle. Shape 4 has the fulcrum above the middle, almost at the top, and Shape 6 has the fulcrum lower than the middle, almost at the bottom. Neither of these horizontal reinforcement levers is in balance. Compared with Shapes 4 and 6, this reinforcement lever (see Figure 15.6) is in balance. The improvements you should make are less radical.

Compare your scores on the principles with the maximum scores and determine where improvements are needed for both foundation and engagement. Determine where you scored lowest in both sections and select some quick wins. It is important to work on both areas at the same time. If you only improve foundation or only improve engagement, you lose the balance and your shape will be different. When you work on them simultaneously, the horizontal lever will change into Shape 1, and you keep the fulcrum in the middle.

Shape 4

This is a horizontal lever far above the middle. If your reinforcement lever looks like Figure 15.7, you need to motivate your learners continuously. Although your program is perfectly focused on the phases of behavioral change, all

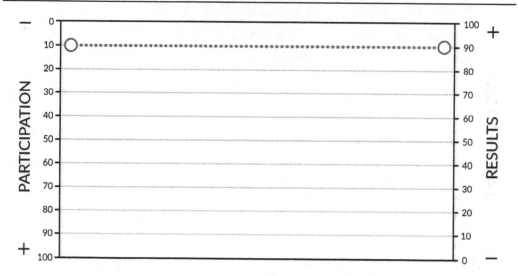

Figure 15.7. Learners in This Reinforcement Program Need More Engagement

reinforcement gaps are taken care of, and a solid measurement plan is included, you will have problems keeping learners engaged and participating.

Your learners don't see the value and don't recognize themselves in your reinforcement program. They don't feel challenged; their brains go into lazy mode. The learners are frustrated or bored because the challenges are not a good fit with their skills level or needs. Check Table 15.2 to see where your score is compared with the maximum score. Focus your development on Principles 4, 5, and 6.

After you complete all your improvements, retake the engagement assessments. You may be able to create Shape 2, or even Shape 1.

Shape 5

The reinforcement lever in Figure 15.8 shows a declining line instead of a rising one. Remember, always strive for a rising line. Compare this figure with Shape 4; this reinforcement lever reflects a program with no focus on results and low participation. This reinforcement program will have a huge dropout rate at the beginning. Learners are not inspired by the program; they don't see any value to spending time on this reinforcement program; and it's not activating their brains.

Perhaps learners experience the measurements as an assessment tool; in other words, they think measurements are for the organization and won't help them apply new skills and knowledge. They don't feel a personal touch, and because the program is not based on a strong foundation, the learners don't

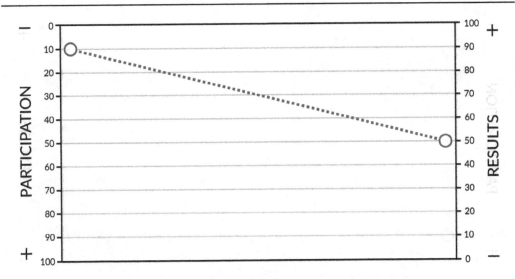

Figure 15.8.   A Reinforcement Program with Low Participation

feel it will help them change their behavior. This program needs extensive adjustments.

A good reinforcement lever is rising, not declining.

Check your scores against the maximum scores for all assessments. Start with your analysis of the principles related to engagement (Principles 4, 5, and 6) because you already have some high scores on the foundation. By improving engagement you can help your reinforcement lever to become more horizontal, which is required to change a declining line into a rising line. Read the suggestions on what you can do to reach a more horizontal line, like Shape 3. Work on the position of the fulcrum by checking some quick wins in Principles 1, 2, or 3.

Don't ignore the messages behind this shape. If you start with this reinforcement program, you will have a hard time. It must be redesigned.

Shape 6

Shape 6 and Shape 4 have the same horizontal line. The difference is that in Shape 6 in Figure 15.9, the line is far below the middle. If your reinforcement lever looks like this, you did a good job on your engagement. The learners will experience a personal program where their brains need to work. However, the program will experience a huge dropout rate later. If people don't

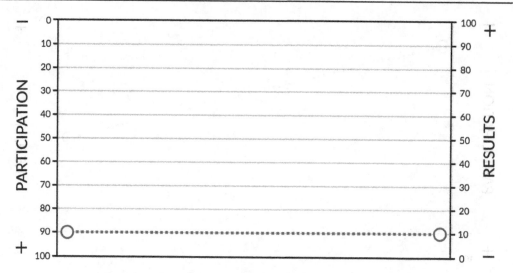

Figure 15.9.   A Reinforcement Program with Good Participation but Limited Progress

obtain results or don't see any progress, they start to question the benefit of the program.

The difference between Shape 6 and Shape 5 is the timing of dropout. In Shape 5 a high percentage of dropouts takes place in the beginning of the program; in this Shape 6, the dropout happens later.

When using this program, don't let the first period of time mislead you. Monitor the participation carefully, even when your score is almost the maximum. Improve all three principles for foundation (Principles 1, 2, and 3).

Shape 7

First check whether you are holding this book upside down. Just kidding. If the shape of your reinforcement lever looks like the one in Figure 15.10, don't expect any results or participation. Although the angle of inclination is 45 degrees exactly, the line is declining. For an effective reinforcement program, you need a rising line.

This shape typically occurs when you break your training materials into pieces and use them as reminders to your learners. A successful reinforcement program is much more than that. It's not a reminder program, and it's not retraining. It's a well-thought-out process of perfectly balanced messages that drive behavior change to create impact in your organization.

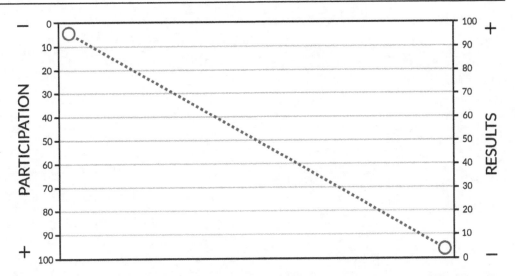

Figure 15.10. A Reinforcement Program with No Participation and No Results

Don't waste your learners' valuable time and hope to achieve some results from this reinforcement program. The only thing you will get is low participation.

You can check your foundation and engagement assessment scores, but you already know the outcome. There are no shortcuts in top-level sports, and there are no shortcuts in reinforcement training.

CHAPTER 16

Crafting Reinforcement Messages

In Judo, the coach has a place close to the *tatami* (mat). During a fight, the coach can give you tips or advice. If a certain fight plan does not work, the coach can make changes and let you know, or he can provide some motivational words if the fighter needs some encouragement. It's great that your coach is that close to you during a fight. The downside is that the coach can only talk during a break.

When I started a fight, my coach was quiet. He observed my moves, analyzed my behavior, and saw what I needed to change. When I competed, a Judo fight lasted five minutes. The referee could decide to have a short break during the fight. Sometimes the break would be only a few seconds; sometimes it would be 15 to 20 seconds. The coach could talk to me only during these breaks—not much time for a full explanation or lots of words.

Every conversation during a fight had to be short, clear, and to the point so I knew exactly what to do. The coach never knew if or when another break would come. So when my coach said, "Turn your hand," I knew exactly what he meant. We used short expressions because they didn't require any additional explanation.

While I was injured in 1990, my coach told me to observe my competitors' coaches during fights. They all had different styles. The top coaches were very precise in their coaching during the breaks. Coaches who lacked experience tried to say too much during a five-second break. They started to explain why it was important to turn your hand. That explanation should have been done prior to the fight. This was not the moment for retraining. Or coaches gave useless information like "one minute to go" although there was a big clock that every fighter could see.

Besides the work my coach did to build a strong foundation, build the team around me, and keep me engaged for many years, his strength was in the short, to-the-point messages during the fights, just like many other top coaches in the world.

Does your reinforcement program communicate like a world-class coach?

After you have built a strong reinforcement program and determined your series of messages, it's time to focus on the details—writing the reinforcement messages itself. As my brother Kees always said, "Become a champion by doing the details extremely well."

In this chapter, you will learn how to write good reinforcement messages. The key is to use short messages, like a top Judo coach does. We'll point out common pitfalls and provide an assessment to see how strong your reinforcement messages are.

THE S.A.F.E. METHOD OF MESSAGES

When you write reinforcement messages, use the S.A.F.E. method. The S.A.F.E. method incorporates four elements that will help you write powerful reinforcement messages:

- Style.
- Active.
- Focus.
- Easy to read.

The following sections explain each of these elements.

Style

When you focus on style, you are writing personally to each learner, and the learner is touched by your messages. To be successful, you must use the correct style to connect with the learner. As you already know, Principle 5, "Create Friction and Direction," keeps the brain active. Everything you do should be focused on keeping the brain alert. Your learner must experience every message as if it were written specifically for him or her.

Write in the second person

As a reinforcement specialist, you know to always write in the second person. Wording like "Your market," "Your learner," "Your development," or "What do you see on. . .?" and "How do you use . . . ?" is much more personalized than messages that use "The market," "Our learner," "The development," or "What we see is. . . ."

Choose your words carefully

Another element of style is the way you emphasize certain topics. Your word choices influence whether a learner is touched by your message. Common mistakes are to say things like "Remember that . . ." or "You must focus on . . ." or "It's important to use. . . ." in your reinforcement messages. Limit the use of these words or expressions. If something is not important or is not helping your learners in their personal development, don't say it.

It's the same as coaching during a Judo fight. My coach never used words like "It's important" when he wanted me to change my approach during a fight. He just emphasized the core message.

Avoid "remember"

The word *remember* is a special word in reinforcement. We always like to limit its use. You don't need this verb to tell your brain to remember a certain topic.

For example, let's say that during your classroom training the facilitator trained your learners on a three-step model of how to overcome objections in a negotiation. In your reinforcement program, you want to reinforce this three-step model and create a nice series of messages. Let's see what happens with the brain if one of your messages starts with the word *remember.*

> "Remember the three-step model from your training. Don't mix these steps, and be sure to follow the correct order."

Seems good. The brain remembers the model, and you give focus points. Short and to the point, correct? Let's see what happens with the brain in the next example.

> "Follow the correct order of the three-step model."

Do you think the brain will work hard to remember the three-step model? Yes, of course. It doesn't need the verb "remember" to remember.

Let's look at another example that combines the use of the verb "remember" and the expression "it's important."

> "Remember the three-step model from your training. It's important that you don't mix these steps, and you must follow the correct order."

This is what is called an "off-the-cuff" message. The writer did not spend a lot of time on the preparation and used simple words to emphasize the message.

Use assumptions

A third element that belongs in the style category is the use of assumptions. In your message, you assume that your learner is already showing certain behavior.

I like to challenge and stimulate the brain by using assumptions that encourage the learner to think.

- As a successful coach, you know . . .
- As a professional salesperson, you use . . .
- As a great leader, you focus on . . .
- As a unique person, you know it's important to . . .

These examples tell the learners nicely that if they want to be successful coaches, they must know. . . , or if they want to be professional salespeople, they need to use. . . . .

By teasing the learners a bit, you stimulate their brains. Challenge your learners and stimulate that thinking process. Let your learners decide whether they fit the assumptions you've made about them.

Active

As a successful reinforcement specialist, you know (recognize this one?) that your learners' brains are lazy and they should be activated all the time.

When using the S.A.F.E. method, the active element is crucial for each of your messages. Lots of learning materials don't have any active element. The facilitator brings the training materials alive and interacts with your learners during training events. If you use your training materials one on one in your messages, you create a lack of brain activity. You can make three important improvements while using training materials:

- Use an active bulleted list.
- Combine assignments and deadlines.
- Use media to activate the memory system.

Use an active bulleted list

Bulleted lists are used in classroom training, on slide decks during a presentation, or in workbooks for learners. Bulleted lists can be used to:

- Summarize points.
- Show the importance of a topic.

- Explain certain steps.
- Draw attention to certain points.
- Provide an overview.

Let's take a closer look at bulleted points by using an example. This summary of points taken from a slide deck used in a classroom event explains key elements of active listening. Assume that the content used in this example is right. I know we could have long discussions about this topic, but focus on the active element rather than the content.

Active listening includes:

- **Acknowledging:** Intention is to show you understand.
- **Paraphrasing:** Summarize or repeat, in your own words, the content of what was said.
- **Empathizing:** Reflect your understanding of what the other person is feeling and the reason for the feeling.
- **Clarifying:** Probe to find out more about what the person said or why she said it.

What is wrong with this list? Nothing. The content is solid and it's part of the training event. But as a reinforcement message, it is not strong. It fails to address what the learner needs to do. It doesn't activate the learner's brain to see this list. It doesn't explain how the learner should transfer this list into his daily work and start using it.

Two key improvements can activate learners' brains:

1. Use numbers or letters. Brains remember numbers and letters much better than they do icons or acronyms.
2. Always ask learners to do something with the list.

Ask learners to do something with a list of points.

What can learners do with a list of points? Some examples of questions to ask include:

1. Which one is the most important?
2. Which order should they be in?

3. What are your top two?

4. What is most difficult and why?

5. Which one have you already mastered?

6. Rank all items.

7. Which one did you work on last week?

8. Select one you will work on next week.

9. Which one would your coach indicate as your need for improvement? Which one would you select for improvement?

Combine assignments and deadlines

In your reinforcement program, use lots of assignments. However, an assignment without a deadline does not trigger the brain to move. If you add a deadline, the brain subconsciously knows that an action is required.

An example of a poor assignment:

Use the active listening model to help your team achieve business results.

Are you triggered to start using this active listening model? No. Learners will read this message and leave it for what it is. This message does not create the behavior change and impact that you want to achieve with your reinforcement program.

Always add a deadline or occasion to an assignment:

For the next week ...

During the next three meetings ...

The next two days ...

In your next sales call ...

Your occasions or deadlines will trigger the learners' brains because our brains are used to timestamps. Keeping track of time is one of the brain's most important tasks. As the brain processes the flood of sights and sounds it encounters, it must also remember when each event occurred. But how does that happen? How does your brain recall that you brushed your teeth before you took a shower, and not the other way around?

For decades, neuroscientists have theorized that the brain timestamps events as they happen, allowing us to keep track of where we are in time and when past events occurred. Your brain timestamps everything and makes recalling events easy: you go back through your timestamps until you see which ones are associated with the event. This also occurs for assignments in the future. Our brains know when and where they need to be completed.

If you want to trigger your learners' memories for an assignment, combine it with an occasion or specific timestamp. A deadline achieves two things:

1. **It forces your learners to think about what it will take to accomplish the assignment.** The learners need to think through the steps they need to achieve the goal. Each step requires a certain amount of time.
2. **Specific assignments help learners prioritize what they work on and for how long.**

Do you remember all the papers and projects you were assigned in school? You had to push yourself to finish everything—and sometimes stayed awake all night to finish an important paper. If we didn't have deadlines with consequences, we would never push ourselves. The same is true for us as reinforcement specialists. We need to set deadlines for learners so they will push themselves.

A common mistake I see in reinforcement programs is an assignment that is too ambitious. It's hard to estimate how long it will take to complete an assignment. Use Principle 7, "Place the Learner in the Center," to think through the time required. Use the DO-DID-GO approach to help the learners accomplish the assignments before they are evaluated.

While writing your reinforcement messages, you can combine style and active elements to make your messages more powerful:

- As a successful coach (style), focus this week (active) on. . . .
- Like a great leader (style), you inspire your team during the next three meetings (active) with. . . .
- Rank this list (active) like a professional salesperson would (style).

Tip: Do not exaggerate. Remain credible.

Use media to activate the memory system

You already know about the relationship between memory and the brain's energy and what role that relationship plays in learning (refer to Chapter 2). Memory allows us to update our knowledge and avoid mistakes. In the classroom or during an e-learning event, when you offer learners a novel environment, their brains scan the space, absorbing information. They must *think* in those situations, which generates memories that are easier to access during reinforcement. If memories are created via mnemonics (visual or verbal), you can use these to activate them. If you write your reinforcement messages, re-use these images, models, or phrases.

I see media used in many reinforcement programs. As you are selecting the media, ask yourself, "What value does it add to my program?" Avoid answers like "It looks nice," "Without it, the message seems so boring," or "Images are always good for engagement."

Every phrase or media piece must have a function to improve the impact of your reinforcement program. Place the learner in the center. How does your choice help learners apply what they have learned? Remember that each phase of behavior change (Awareness, Knowledge/Skills, and Apply) needs different follow-up.

Not all media are suitable in a reinforcement message. Don't retrain.

A good way to determine the key images or phrases is to write down what you can remember. Select a training or e-learning event you want to reinforce and write down the images and phrases you consider key:

_____

_____

_____

_____

_____

_____

_____

_____

_____

If you feel your involvement in designing the reinforcement program prevents you from having a realistic overview, talk to 10 learners from the pilot group that went through the training event. What do they consider a key image or phrase? Use their answers as you write the reinforcement messages. Ask for their input within a week after the training. As you know, people start to forget as soon as they leave the classroom. The Ebbinghaus Forgetting Curve shows that people forget 70 percent of their training after 24 hours.

Focus

Reinforcement messages are short, to the point, and help your learners transfer learning into application. Reinforcement is not retraining and not sending as much content to the learners as possible in the hope they will use it. Any extra information in each reinforcement message needs to be eliminated.

No single message creates behavior change. The entire series of messages creates behavior change. Each message has a specific role in that process.

If you have finished your design of the reinforcement program and your reinforcement lever has a good shape, you can complete your messages. Trust the series and write every single message to conform to the S.A.F.E. method. Then the messages will do the work.

It's more difficult to reduce content and text than to add everything you have available.

In your reinforcement program, create instructions that will take no more than two minutes for the learners to complete. You don't have to write complete instructions for a new digital workbook. Avoid mixing reinforcement and additional learning materials. I recommend an adaptive program to split the reinforcement and additional learning materials.

When you work on focus, place the learner in the center and always consider how to add value for him or her. Challenge yourself, asking: "What is the minimum my learner needs in this phase?"

When you check your messages for "the minimum," remove any excess text, even if it's only one word. Determine the purpose of the message and delete all side issues. A good test is to check whether the key message will change if you delete extra information. If it won't, delete it!

Use specific titles

If you use titles for your messages, use no more than 25 characters. What is the essence of each message? Don't write complete sentences to explain what the message is about. Learners can scan through your titles and find the topics they want in the messages. Titles like "question" or "assignment" are not specific enough.

Ask one question at a time

You will also want some introductions to questions. In Principle 3, "Create Measurable Behavior Change," we introduced a measurement plan that relies on good questions.

I have reviewed many designers' introductions and questions, and I always find the same mistakes. The content is correct, but the message is confusing. Imagine if my Judo coach had asked me questions like these after a fight or training:

- "Did you feel strong, or was he stronger?"
- "Did you follow your diet and drink enough water?"
- "How did your weight training go, and did you see any progress?"
- "When is your next training, and what is your goal for that training?"

I probably would have had a hard time answering him, not because I didn't know the answer but because the question was complex. What was the coach looking for? Don't make it hard for your learner to answer. Avoid asking two questions at the same time. Focus on what you want to ask. One question per topic.

Make the questions specific

Another point is to avoid misunderstanding because the question is not specific enough. The one question you ask should be specific. You probably recognize these examples of open-field questions:

- What are your current struggles as a coach?
- What do you think are the differences between steps?
- Are those behaviors already in your action plan?
- How important is active listening to business results?

What do you think your learner will answer? How can you help learners to answer at their best? Take for example the first question "What are your current struggles as a coach?" It's a good open-ended question; after all, it starts with "What."

However, the rest of the question is too general. Is your learner struggling with finding a good parking spot each morning? Is your learner having troubles in his marriage? Is the learner not satisfied with the team's performance? What struggles does the learner experience while applying new knowledge and skills? It's up to the learner what the answer will be. Unless you use open-ended questions with multiple-choice answers, you cannot guide the learner's answer. Unless you use open-ended questions for self-reflection, ask more precise questions.

Focus your reinforcement program on open-ended questions that require hard thinking, need evidence to answer the question, and elicit answers that have depth. Use questions that cannot be searched online and focus on the result or effect of the application.

- What is the impact. . .?
- What is the influence. . .?
- What is the relationship. . .?
- What if. . .?
- What would happen. . .?
- What could happen. . .?
- What is the result. . .?
- How can you apply. . .?
- What is the cause of. . .?
- What is the effect of. . .?
- How can you change or modify. . .?
- What could you do to improve. . .?
- How can you ensure that. . .?
- What might happen if. . .?

Open-ended questions should be used to promote critical thinking and otherwise create intellectual involvement.

If you use closed questions in your reinforcement program, make sure these questions always add value to the learners. A technically perfect closed question can be worthless. A closed question like "Do you understand?" is technically a good closed question, but it adds zero value for your learners. There are better ways to figure out whether a learner understands the knowledge or skills necessary for behavior change. Also, asking whether something has been done does not give you any insight on quality.

Avoid focusing on quantity

I have reviewed many reinforcement programs created by specialists in L&D departments in big organizations. These specialists all like to measure *quantity*: "How many meetings did you have last week?" or "How many times did you speak with your team?" or "How many. . .?" Or they even ask closed questions like "Did you have a meeting today?"

These questions are valuable for the organization to collect data, but how do they use Principle 7, "Place the Learner in the Center"? Questions about quantity are not wrong, but you must combine them with quality questions about your reinforcement program to receive meaningful answers and provide more depth for your analysis.

Easy to Read

The fourth element of the S.A.F.E. Model is all about helping the learners and avoiding misunderstandings. When you write your messages, you need to think about the learners. Is the message easy to read, easy to understand, and easy to use?

Challenge yourself and see whether you have met two criteria:

1. The average length of your message is 400 characters.
2. Each sentence has a maximum of 17 words.

Craft short messages

It's not easy writing reinforcement messages with a limit of 400 characters. Besides skipping all extra words, you also meet all of the other S.A.F.E. Model elements, like adding deadlines to assignments or using bulleted lists. Writing good, short reinforcement messages require lots of practices.

I set a limit of 400 characters for messages because this length keeps the attention of an average learner. You don't want to lose their attention while they are reading your messages. Many writers claim that the average person's attention span is only eight seconds, one second shorter than a goldfish's attention span. Because holding a learner's attention is an important element for good reinforcement results, I have spent quite a bit of time studying attention spans.

I cannot believe that my attention span during a fight was only eight seconds. What would happen if it were only eight seconds? Some trainings lasted two hours and, even then, I did not lose my focus. So where does the eight seconds come from? And what is attention anyway?

Other research shows support for a variable attention span far longer than eight seconds and dependent on many factors. Think about your own attention span. Can you watch a movie or read a book and pay attention longer than eight seconds?

Attention levels

Wilson and Korn (2007) did a literature review in which they discussed many flaws in the research on attention span during learning. They concluded that attention span varies and that it is impossible to offer a specific estimate for how long people can pay attention.

If you want to make maximum use of learners' attention span, you first need to know what attention is. Some say attention is the ability to focus on one thing and not become distracted by other things in the environment. But that's just one part of attention. Your learners can't remember or process information that they don't attend to. Attention is critical for learning, and memory and attention are related.

According to Sohlberg and Mateer's Attention Model (2001), there are five levels of attention, as shown in Table 16.1.

While we are learning something, the world around us bombards us with stimuli that could overwhelm us in a learning environment. So, the brain must filter most of this out so we are not overloaded. As a reinforcement specialist, you know that your learner cannot learn or successfully apply what they have learned while they are overloaded.

Table 16.1. Levels of Attention

Level	Description
1. Focused (easiest level)	Response to external stimuli. **Example:** reacting when touched.
2. Sustained	Ongoing focus to carry out repetitive tasks. **Example:** Remembering instructions and carrying them out when needed.
3. Selective	Staying focused while distractions are present. **Example:** Performing tasks while there are distractions such as noise and movement
4. Alternating	Shifting focus between tasks that need different skills. **Example:** Alternating between asking questions, listening for the answers, and typing in facts on a form
5. Divided (most difficult level)	Responding simultaneously to multiple tasks (may be rapid switching of alternating attention) **Example:** Talking on the phone while sending an email.

Types of attention

In addition to levels of attention, Chun, Golumb, and Turk-Browne (2011) describe two *types* of attention:

- **External attention** refers to how we select and process information through our senses from the world.
- **Internal attention** refers to how we select and process information from inside, such as memory and feelings.

If your learners change their behavior, that is, learn and apply what they have learned, both types of attention are involved. When reading your reinforcement messages, your learners are processing information from outside, using their working memory and linking outside information to "information" from inside (including thoughts, feelings, and what they already know).

Attention is complex. There is likely no set attention span, so there's no need to write your reinforcement messages for a tiny, eight-second attention span. But you do need to gain and keep learners' attention during training because internal and external stimuli compete for attention all the time. So, keep your messages short with an average length of 400 characters.

If you analyze your reinforcement programs for which there are less-than-desirable outcomes, look for attention difficulties. For example, are you expecting your learners to do too many things at once (Level 5) or to do things in situations in which there are a lot of distractions (Level 3)?

Principle 2, "Close the 5 Reinforcement Gaps," shows you the five areas to consider while building your foundation. One of them is the environment. A part of the environment is the knowing the attention level that's going to be possible.

Use short sentences

Another topic that relates to easy to read is *readability*. The Flesch-Kincaid Readability Test is probably the most commonly cited and used. The test uses a mathematical formula to determine how easily readers will understand the text:

- Sentence length as judged by the average number of words in a sentence.
- Word length as judged by the average number of syllables in a word.

Table 16.2. Flesch-Kincaid Readability Scores

Grade	Average Syllables/Word	Average sentence length
Kindergarten	1.5	10 words
3 to 5	1.6	14 words
6 to 8	**1.6**	**15 words**
College/University	1.85	19 to 23 words

The rationale is straightforward. Sentences that contain a lot of words are more difficult to follow than shorter sentences. Similarly, words that contain a lot of syllables are harder to read than words with fewer syllables. Aim for 8th-grade level, understood by 13- to 14-year-olds, using the Flesch-Kincaid Readability Tests as a guide.

Challenge yourself to use a maximum of 17 words per sentence. This will help you to reach the average sentence length of 15 words at 8th-grade level. Avoid constructions with lots of lengthy phrases. It's better to use two separate sentences than a long, convoluted sentence. Count your words and rewrite if needed. Make it a habit, a game, and your goal.

Use Table 16.2 to check your readability score and how well you are achieving your goal to reach the 8th-grade level.

S.A.F.E. Model Assessment

As a reinforcement specialist, your reinforcement messages are like my coach's instructions were during the short breaks in my Judo fights. He didn't have a lot of time to give me instructions. He could give me only useful information, offer one tip at the time, activate learning created during our training sessions, inspire me, and address me in the second person. He used the S.A.F.E. model to the max.

How well are you using the S.A.F.E. model to craft your messages? Use the assessment below to find improvements you could make. Check your reinforcement messages. If you meet the criteria, give yourself 1 point for yes and 0 points for no in the Y/N column.

(continued)

(continued)

Then multiply the number in the Y/N column by the number in the Weight column and sum the numbers. The total score indicates your use of the S.A.F.E. model.

Criteria	Y/N	Weight	Y/N × Weight
Is the message written in the second person?		3	
Is all excess text skipped?		2	
Is your bulleted list active case?		3	
Did you avoid words like "remember"?		1	
Did you avoid words like "it's important"?		1	
Does every assignment have a time element?		3	
Does the medium you use activate the learners' memories?		2	
Does each item contain only one question?		3	
Is the introduction to the question specific?		2	
Did you avoid using the words "you must"?		1	
Is the question specific?		2	
Is the average length of the message under 400 characters?		2	
Is the text inspiring to the learner?		2	
Is the maximum length of a sentence 17 words?		2	
Does the title of your message reflect the essence of its content?		1	
Total score			

Check your score. If your total score is:

Less than 13 points: we advise a *no go* and rewrite

14 to 19 points: needs improvement

20 to 24 points: needs attention

25 to 30 points: ready to go

To analyze more in detail and determine which element of the S.A.F.E model you can improve on, use the following list to see what criteria reflects what S.A.F.E. model element.

Criteria	S.A.F.E Model
Is the message written in the second person?	Style
Is all excess text skipped?	Focus
Is your bulleted list active case?	Active
Did you avoid words like "remember"?	Style
Did you avoid words like "it's important"?	Style
Does every assignment have a time element?	Active
Does the medium you use activate the learners' memories?	Active
Does each item contain only one question?	Focus
Is the introduction to the question specific?	Focus
Did you avoid using the words "you must"?	Style
Is the question specific?	Focus
Is the average length of the message under 400 characters?	Easy to Read
Is the text inspiring to the learner?	Easy to Read
Is the maximum length of a sentence 17 words?	Easy to Read
Does the title of your message reflect the essence of its content?	Focus

(You can find a copy of this assessment in the Appendix of this book.)

CHAPTER 17

Reinforcement for Different Training Types

"**C**an I use The 7 Principles for all types of training?" is a question we some-times hear. Maybe you wonder the same thing. The answer is simple: "Yes." However, each training type has need for a specific type of reinforcement program. In this chapter, we will discuss ten different training types and their specific reinforcement approaches.

TRAINING TYPES

Before you know how to reinforce your training, you have to know what type of training you're providing your learners. Here is a quick overview of common training programs:

1. Soft skills.
2. Technical/knowledge.
3. Cultural programs.
4. Awareness training (such as safety).
5. Certification.
6. On-boarding.
7. Coaching.
8. Refresher training (retraining).
9. Educational (such as MBA).
10. Compliance training.

Compare yours training types with this list. Are any training types you use missing? Look at Table 17.1 to understand each training type. Table 17.2 shows where you should focus your attention in the reinforcement program for each type of training.

Table 17.1. Types of Training

Training Type	Description
Soft Skills	Soft skills are a cluster of productive personality traits that characterize one's relationships in a milieu. These skills can include social graces, communication abilities, personal habits, cognitive or emotional empathy, time management, teamwork, and leadership traits.
Technical/ Knowledge	Technical training teaches the skills and knowledge needed to design, develop, implement, maintain, support, or operate a particular technology or related application, product, or service.
Cultural Programs	Culture training is mostly focused on awareness, accountability, and culture change. Implementing and adopting positive culture change often aligns with high-level business goals.
Awareness Training	Awareness training increases learners' understanding of the importance of a certain topic and the adverse consequences of not implementing it.
Certification	Training and a formal procedure by which you assess and verify the attributes, characteristics, quality, qualification, or "status" of your learners. Attests to knowledge in writing by issuing a certificate.
On-Boarding	On-boarding is introducing a new learner to the organization and its procedures, rules and regulations, and the new job. It is often short and informative.
Coaching	Coaching is focused on the relationship between a coach and the person being coached. The coach is there to help someone meet a specific goal. Once the goal is met, the relationship is usually terminated.
Refresher Training (Retraining)	The purpose of refresher training is to acquaint learners with the latest methods of performing their jobs and improve their efficiency. Often used to avoid obsolescence or when newly created jobs are given to existing learners.
Educational	Education is all about learning theory. Traditionally, education may reinforce knowledge in which you already have a foundation. Training gives your learners the skills to do something, rather than just know about something. In educational programs the learners develop a foundation upon which to build skills
Compliance Training	Compliance training refers to the process of educating your learners on laws, regulations, and company policies that apply to their day-to-day job responsibilities.

Some of the reinforcement principles are better suited to some training programs than others. Table 17.2 offers suggestions for which principles to focus on as you design a reinforcement program for the training you've presented to learners. Where gamification and scenarios are mentioned, refer to the corresponding sections later in this chapter for an explanation of how to incorporate these into your reinforcement program.

Table 17.2. Reinforcements for Training Types

Training Type	Attention Points for Reinforcement
Soft Skills	• Because soft skills can be very broad, spend enough time to determine the reinforcement objectives.
Technical/ Knowledge	• Spend relatively more time on knowledge components.
	• Provide your learners with additional learning materials.
	• Check regularly whether your learners are comfortable with their current knowledge levels.
	• Consider a longer reinforcement program (12 months) to guarantee technical updates.
	• Integrate a technical library.
	• Pay a lot of attention to Principle 6, "Follow the Reinforcement Flow."
	• You can use gamification to drive engagement.
Cultural Programs	• Spend at least 50 percent of your time on awareness.
	• Challenge the learner with the "Why?" questions.
	• Emphasize what the learners can do, and apply the new culture.
	• In Principle 2, "Close the 5 Reinforcement Gaps," emphasize the Motivation Gap.
	• Use Principle 3, "Create Measurable Behavior Change," to gain insights on opinions. Avoid building an assessment tool.
	• Use Principle 5, "Create Friction and Direction," to inspire the learners to make connections across all culture topics.
	• This reinforcement program may be less suitable for gamification.
	• Use lots of scenarios for learners to reflect on.
Awareness Training	• The reinforcement objectives can be topics that your learners may not use or situations that never occur. But if they occur, the knowledge and skills they learn must be accurate. Therefore, use lots of "what-if" scenarios.
	• If you use the scenarios, pay a lot of attention to Principle 6, "Follow the Reinforcement Flow."

(continued)

Table 17.2. *(Continued)*

Training Type	Attention Points for Reinforcement
	• Consider a longer, more adaptive reinforcement program (12 months) and let the learners select topics of interest.
	• See also reinforcement suggestions for culture programs.
	• Use Principle 4, "Provide the Perfect Push and Pull," to guarantee continued communication with your learners.
	• Is the organization culture suitable for gamification? For this reinforcement program a team leader board can be motivational. Keep the learners engaged and stimulate talking to each other.
Certification	• In this reinforcement program, your focus is on assessments. Use Principle 4, "Provide the Perfect Push and Pull," and focus on Pull.
	• No need to provide additional learning materials.
	• Create a continuous measurement program. Instead of one set of 25 questions all at once, spread them out over five weeks.
	• Use check questions to discover learners' real knowledge levels. Avoid asking the same questions. If you do, you are not measuring knowledge, but whether learners remember the correct answers. Your reinforcement program should not focus on remembering.
On-Boarding	• In this reinforcement program the percentage of time spent on awareness can be minimal. The program needs to provide information and an explanation.
	• Use additional information for your learners.
	• Consider a longer reinforcement program (six months) and let the learners continuously work on all topics.
	• Taper off the frequency after three months, but keep measuring.
	• Use Principle 4, "Provide the Perfect Push and Pull," to track learners' progress and understanding of all new items.
	• This program may be not suitable for gamification, but reward completion.
Coaching	• This reinforcement program is not a soft skill program where your learners need to apply coaching skills. This is a program to reinforce a coach who coaches other people.
	• The frequency of your reinforcement messages can be less frequent. Perhaps one message every two weeks.

Training Type	Attention Points for Reinforcement
	• Close all gaps using Principle 2, "Close the 5 Reinforcement Gaps."
	• Use Principles 3, "Create Measurable Behavior Change," to let the coaches think and evaluate their roles and added value.
	• Use Principle 5, "Create Friction and Direction," to let coaches think.
	• This program is not suitable for gamification.
Refresher Training (Retraining)	• This reinforcement program is a good place for assessments and summaries of learning content.
	• Emphasize the Why? in Principle 1, "Master the 3 Phases of Behavior Change."
	• Use Principle 4, "Provide the Perfect Push and Pull" to gain insights about what their current levels of knowledge are.
	• Pay a lot of attention to Principle 6, "Follow the Reinforcement Flow."
	• The use of realistic scenarios will drive learner engagement.
	• This reinforcement program is suitable for gamification.
Educational	• In this reinforcement program, you can use pre- and post-reinforcement.
	• Use Principle 3, "Create Measurable Behavior Change," to measure how solid your learners' "foundations" are before developing their skills levels.
	• Pay a lot of attention to Principle 6, "Follow the Reinforcement Flow."
	• This reinforcement program is suitable for gamification.
Compliance Training	• Emphasize the Awareness in Principle 1, "Master the 3 Phases of Behavior Change," and explain the "Why?"
	• Close all gaps in Principle 2, "Close the 5 Reinforcement Gaps."
	• Use Principle 5, "Create Friction and Direction," to avoid a "check off" reinforcement program.
	• Consider a longer, more adaptive reinforcement program (12 months), and let the learners select topics of interest in addition to the required topics.
	• In this reinforcement program, you can use "what-if" scenarios.
	• Stimulate social friction while using Principle 5, "Create Friction and Direction."

MOVING BEYOND THE PRINCIPLES

The 7 Principles are the framework on which to build your reinforcement program. They influence your goals, and you can help your learners to achieve your goals by engaging them through Principles 4, 5, and 6. In addition to the design of your reinforcement program, gamification and scenarios influence engagement. Here are some ways to improve learners' engagement through gaming elements and suggestions for how to use the scenarios for maximum effect.

Gamification

Gamification is the process of adding game-like elements to your reinforcement program to encourage learners' participation. Gamification is different from playing a full-fledged game. Rather, learners engage in an artificial conflict, defined by rules, that results in a quantifiable outcome and behavior change. As Kees says, "With jumping frogs or Tetris, you don't change behavior."

Gamification, on the other hand, uses elements of games such as points and leader boards, high-score tables that indicate an individual or team's performance. Your learners can earn points that can be used to indicate status.

If you decide to use gamification for your reinforcement program, use elements that support the desired behavior change. As a reinforcement specialist, you know that reinforcement messages drive behavior change. Your gamification can focus on those messages. If your learners follow the series of messages you designed, they can collect points. If they don't earn points, they lose, not only the game, but also when applying they concepts in the training.

Each type of reinforcement message has a certain impact on behavior change. A welcome message has less impact then a self-evaluation; a general knowledge question probably will have less effect than a specific question on a key element.

The process is simple: Give each of your reinforcement messages a score between 1 and 100. A score of 1 means less impact on the behavior change and 100 means maximum impact on behavior change. Keep the scoring structure the same across the messages. Use Table 17.3 as a guideline. Feel free to create your own measurement schedule.

Once you assign a weight to every reinforcement message, your "game" can start. If a learner completes an assignment within an acceptable time frame, let's say 48 hours, he or she collects the assigned points. For example, let's say you scheduled a quiz question with the weight of 80 points in the second week on a Wednesday. If a learner answers this question within 48 hours after receiving the message, he or she earns the maximum number of points, in this case 80.

Table 17.3. Message Scoring Examples

Message Type	Weight
Welcome, finish, or structure messages	1 to 20
Quiz questions	50 to 100
Survey questions	40 to 70
Behavior change questions	60 to 100
Reflection questions	50 to 100
Explanation	30 to 60
Assignments	40 to 70
Pitfalls	50 to 80
DO-DID-GO	40–70–90

If he or she completes this question after two weeks, fewer points are awarded, in this case 20.

The points that a learner receives are based on Principle 6, "Follow the Reinforcement Flow." The better a learner follows the design, the higher the score. For the "game," all scores are added up and you can reward the learner with the highest score, who followed your design best. You can also add bonus points if a quiz question is answered correctly or if a learner completed the assignment within 24 hours. All is driven by series of messages you create based on The 7 Principles of Reinforcement.

If you have multiple learners who follow your reinforcement program and all of them collect points, you can set up a leader board. This allows you to rank the learners or to combine scores and rank teams or departments. Based on this ranking, you can appoint winners and give prizes or incentives. This type of leader board can drive participation.

Reinforcement programs with a gamification strategy motivate learners and drive more engagement. We see that three out of four learners in a gamified environment are motivated to invest more effort in learning and applying what they learn. However, make sure that the gamification you select fits the organization culture. Not every culture or function is suitable for gamification. On the contrary, it can be counterproductive.

Scenarios

Scenarios are used in many reinforcement programs and can be very effective, especially in Culture, Awareness, or Compliance reinforcement programs.

Simply telling your learners what to do does not always work. Learning from real-life examples maximizes learner engagement and knowledge retention.

Learners often retain information better through a story or a scenario that they can relate to than from lectures and speeches. Stories inspire and motivate learners, who then try to emulate the characters in the stories. Scenarios or role plays place your learners in realistic situations and urge them to use skills and information they have acquired to respond to what is happening.

If you consider using scenarios, your will need to do two things:

1. Write concrete scenarios that are both believable and effective.
2. Use questions that are effective for your reinforcement program.

Use the following guidelines to create believable and effective scenarios:

1. **Understand your learners:** You must understand your learners and know their needs and expectations. Know the skills they already possess, the extent of challenge that can be given to them, and the outcome that they want. Not understanding the learners might result in a scenario too boring or too complex to achieve your desired results.

2. **Create relevant situations:** A scenario is essentially a story with characters and situations, usually accompanied by questions that challenge your learners to respond. Make your scenarios as real as possible. Unless the learners find them believable and relevant, they will not relate to them. Only a realistic situation can engage learners and help them retain useful information.

3. **Follow reinforcement flow:** If you follow the reinforcement flow, your scenario should motivate the learners to action. A scenario must pose a problem for your learners to respond to by recalling their previous knowledge. Thus, an effective scenario motivates learners to believe that they have the necessary knowledge and skills to overcome any problems they encounter.

4. **Challenge learners:** Only when learners face some sort of challenging situation and must think of a solution will a scenario be effective. The best way to write scenarios is to present a problem, provide some clues, and then provide the challenge. Your challenge should not overwhelm your learners or they may not put any effort into finding a solution.

5. **Use the S.A.F.E. method:** As for your reinforcement messages, use the 8th-grade reading level, average of 15 words per sentence, and use an average of 1.6 syllables per word. It also makes a scenario interesting and informal, so learning happens in a natural way.

6. **Employ visual graphics:** A scenario becomes much more effective when it is presented with visuals. Use mnemonics techniques, for example.

Now that you have created believable scenarios, write questions you can use to challenge your learners. Remember to use questions they cannot find answers to online. "What-if" questions are effective, such as:

- What if. . .?
- What might happen if. . .?
- What could you do to. . .?
- How can you. . .?
- What is the result if. . .?

Follow the Focus element of the S.A.F.E. method from Chapter 16 to draft strong scenario questions.

Knowledge vs. knowing

In Table 17.2, I emphasized *knowledge* in the reinforcement programs for Technical, Certification, and Refresher trainings. I used knowledge—not knowing— in the table intentionally because there is a difference between knowing and knowledge.

Knowledge is being able to talk about a topic for an extended period of time using complete and logical sentences. Knowing falls more into the memory category. For example, I *know* what the weather is like outside, but I can't have an in-depth conversation about weather.

You want to measure knowledge, not memory, in your reinforcement program. For that reason, don't use the same questions that were used in training to prove knowledge retention. Use different questions to measure learners' level of knowledge.

Measure knowledge, not memory.

CHAPTER 18

Introducing Your Reinforcement Program

As a reinforcement specialist, you worked hard on your reinforcement programs, you used all 7 principles, created the perfect reinforcement lever, and had a great score on your S.A.F.E. Assessment. What can go wrong?

How you introduce your reinforcement program can create problems.

The success of your reinforcement program begins while your learners are still in the training phase, and your trainers have a large impact on how well the reinforcement program goes.

RELYING ON THE TRAINERS

A classroom trainer is the ambassador for your reinforcement program. It is crucial to the success of your program that a trainer understands the reinforcement process and helps to provide purpose and value. Professional trainers are important stakeholders and can be used in the development process. They can add value when determining reinforcement objectives. Use the 10-step approach and involve the trainers. Use the trainers as a test group or use their expertise early in the development process.

Your reinforcement success relies on each trainer's understanding and implementation of the program. Trainers often don't understand that the reinforcement program does not replace the training. Explain that your reinforcement program is a *continuation* of the training and helps the learners to apply what they have learned.

Even if the trainer has been involved in the design process, do not underestimate his or her role in the learners' on-boarding. You can help the trainer by focusing on two moments: (1) when you finished your design of your reinforcement program (prior to a training event) and (2) at the launch of your program during the training.

The sooner a trainer is involved in your reinforcement program, the better he or she will be able to emphasize the importance of the reinforcement program during the training. Prior to your training event, you should:

- Invite the trainer to participate in the reinforcement program. This will allow the trainer to experience the entire process before any of the learners do.

- Check with your trainer and make sure he or she has a complete understanding of your reinforcement program.

During your training event, your trainer should:

1. **Introduce your reinforcement program at the beginning of the session.** This introduction is meant to trigger the curiosity of the learners and should be short. The trainer should do this at the beginning of the training session because it allows him or her to connect the (classroom) training to your reinforcement program throughout the training sessions.

2. **During relevant moments, the trainer should draw connections between his program and topics in the reinforcement program.** Work with your trainers to determine these moments and what to say. Examples include:
   - "You'll receive a useful video messages on this topic."
   - "There will be several assignments in your reinforcement program covering this topic."
   - "Look for messages in your reinforcement program with a very interesting white paper on this topic."

3. **On the last day of training, have trainers introduce examples of reinforcement messages and explain the reinforcement process.** What objectives did you select? How does reinforcement work? What is a series of messages? Why does this help the learner . . .? This introduction should last about 10 minutes. My best advice is to provide a slide deck that trainers can use or spend time during the e-learning explaining reinforcement.

We see too much misunderstanding during the collaboration between a reinforcement specialist and a trainer. The trainer is unclear about what reinforcement is, the connection between the training event and the reinforcement, and what the reinforcement program involves and how it will help the learners apply what they have learned. This ambiguous situation, combined with an overloaded training event, can lead to the trainer spending only a few minutes at the end of the program introducing your reinforcement program.

You don't want your hard work to be introduced just before the learners are ready to go home as: "Oh yeah, by the way, there is a reinforcement program."

CHAPTER 19

Sore Made

In the summer of 1971, when I was four years old, my parents let me play in the garden behind our house. As little kids do, I liked to discover the world. Of course, I did not always do what my mother told me to do: "Don't play with the flowers." "Stay on the grass." "Don't throw the football over the fence."

The more my mother told me what to do, the more I wondered: "What if I don't show that behavior?" (I probably didn't ask that specific question in those words at that age.)

When my mother told me to do or *not* to do something, I often did the opposite. When she said, "Don't throw your football over the fence," she triggered me to see what would happen if I threw the ball over the fence. And of course, I did.

My mother made it clear that she did not like what she had seen. She told me to go to the neighbor's house, explain what I had done, and ask whether I could get my football back. I knew this was a serious command, so I listened to my mother.

Shy and afraid, I went to the front door of the neighbor's house and rang their bell. When they opened the door, I explained what had happened, and I apologized for my behavior. The neighbor told me I could get my football from the garden behind their house.

When I entered their garden, I saw a wash line where a big white Japanese suit was hanging in the sun. My red plastic football lay under the suit. I was fascinated by the white suit, but I was also afraid to look at the other side of that suit. Was there a mud spot on it from my ball?

The neighbor saw my reaction and explained that the white suit was a Japanese Judo suit. I started to ask questions like: "Why do you have that suit?" "Why do you use it?" "Why is it so white?" "Why? . . . Why? . . . Why?" You know how small kids love to ask questions. They are curious and want to know everything.

The neighbor explained that his son Maarten was a Judo player and member of the national Dutch Judo team. He invited me to meet his son the following weekend. Maarten and I spent many hours after that playing as if we were Japanese fighters in the biggest Judo tournaments in the world.

This is how my behavior changed and I got my start eventually to become a professional Judo player. This book is the latest part of my story.

Please understand this anecdote correctly. Fascination and curiosity about the unknown (Flow Zone) drives possible behavior change. Some people think that because I did not listen to my mother and did not show the desired behavior, those were my start of my behavior change toward becoming a professional Judo player. If that is the secret to successfully changing behavior and creating lasting impact, you don't need The 7 Principles of Reinforcement (just kidding). The daily practice required to change behavior shows the importance of balancing The 7 Principles and keeping the learner in the center.

Behavior change is a *process*. Before we started learning Judo, Kees and I were normal kids who liked to be active. The combination of training and reinforcement transformed us into Judo champions. Without training reinforcement from our coach, we would never have made it to that level.

When it comes to corporate training, solutions offered in the learning industry are good at regurgitating lessons and reminding learners of what they've been taught, but they don't reinforce training events, which is required to change lasting behavior.

Throughout this book, we've used our personal experiences in Judo to inspire you to embrace behavior change. Just as Olympic athletes need a coach and structure, the people whose behavior you are seeking to change need guidance and a methodology. Even the coaches of top athletes use The 7 Principles of Reinforcement to guarantee the transfer of knowledge and skills learned during training into skills executed during competitions.

Do you remember the two questions my coach asked me when he came into that small locker room in 1987? "Do you want to become an Olympic champion?" and "Is it also your choice?" The rest of my life has been a consequence of my answer to the second question.

If I ask, "Do you want to create an effective reinforcement program?" your answer will probably be "Yes, I do." The second question may be more difficult to answer. Answering yes means you must challenge yourself and continually find a perfect balance of The 7 Principles.

You have learned that reinforcement is so much more than cutting your training content into little pieces and sending the pieces to your learners. Your learners' mind-set influences the results of your reinforcement program. You now know how the brain works, why your learners forget, and how to overcome the forgetting curve.

You also understand that behavior change always happens in 3 phases. You cannot skip a phase. Learners respond to each phase differently. If your learners understand *why* they should change, the next question is *how* to change. Only when your learners can answer the *why* and *how* questions can lasting behavior change be achieved.

To help your learners in these phases, you realize the value of repetition, are aware of the power of spaced learning, and know that it's all about sending the right messages at the right time. To determine these messages and their timing, you don't use the training goals, but instead determine the reinforcement objectives. Based on an active verb, you create a series of messages that drives behavior change. The 7 Principles of Reinforcement will help you determine the messages needed for a strong foundation and to drive the engagement needed for results and participation.

Three of the principles support the foundation, and three more support engagement. Can you list these principles without cheating? We hope you can. I will give you the one that is missing. Number 7, Place the Learner in the Center.

If you could list the other six principles and know which ones are used to build the foundation and which ones to build the engagement, I want to compliment you. Well done, even when you needed to think hard.

If you couldn't list all of the principles, don't throw your football over the fence and give up. Flip back to Chapter 5, where you can read an overview of the principles that will help you create lasting behavior change.

However, being able to list the principles does not mean you can apply them. Application means that you start using the principles in your reinforcement program. Check your notes, text highlights, and bookmarks to reinforce what you learned earlier in the book. You only win the gold medal when you execute extremely well.

As in Judo, finding the right balance is important in an effective reinforcement program. A Judo player who is out of balance can hardly win a competition. In fact, a Judo player who is out of balance will probably lose the first fight.

A reinforcement program that is out of balance will probably not result in lasting behavior change. You need to create a balance between results and participation. The balance comes when you build a strong foundation and drive engagement. And, of course, all of this is done while focusing on the learner.

After your reinforcement program has been in place for a while, I recommend that you analyze it and determine where it could be improved. Just as top athletes do when they want to reach the next level, face the facts, confront yourself, dare to grow, and don't be afraid of losing. When most top athletes look back at their sport careers, they conclude that they lost more medals than they won. As my coach told me: "You have to lose medals to win the most important one."

So, don't throw your football over the fence; instead, show top-sport behavior. Check the assessments and reinforcement levers described in Part 4 to determine how well balanced your reinforcement programs are and then revisit the principles on which you fall short to balance your reinforcement program. Remember, lots of reinforcement specialists want to build reinforcement programs, but you must choose to build an *effective* reinforcement program.

Perhaps you wondered about the title of this chapter, "Sore Made." "Sore Made" is what the referee calls to signal the end of a Judo contest. When they hear "Sore Made," both Judo players stop fighting and return to their start positions facing each other. After the referee declares the winner, the players take one step back and bow to their opponents. This bow means "Thank you for this challenge and I respect you as a human being."

I am not sure whether that was my first thought when I lost my Olympic medal, but today I have a good reason to call the last chapter of this book "Sore Made." It represents the bow I make to you, which means thank you for reading our book, thank you for using The 7 Principles, but most of all, I have respect for you! I admire you because you value the importance of behavior change. I wish you the best of luck in achieving it.

APPENDIX

TOOLS FOR BUILDING A

REINFORCEMENT PROGRAM

Step	Steps to Determine Reinforcement Objective	Check
1	Identify Your Top Three Training Goals	☐
2	Determine Desired Training Impact	☐
3	Measure Your Training Goals	☐
4	Outline Reinforcement Objectives	☐
5	Include Measurable Action Verbs	☐
6	Determine Key Takeaways	☐
7	Outline Measurement Plan	☐
8	Close the Knowledge Gap	☐
9	Close the Skill Gap	☐
10	Motivate Your Learners	☐

PRINCIPLE 1. ASSESSMENT

How did the foundation of your reinforcement program perform? Read each statement below and give yourself points based on the scale:

Poor: 1 point

Fair: 2 points

Good: 3 points

Excellent: 4 points

Principle 1: Master the 3 Phases

The ratio is 15 percent Awareness; 25 percent Knowledge and Skills; 60 percent Apply	
Awareness is focused on *why*	
Knowledge/Skills are focused *how*	
Apply is focused on the DO-DID-GO approach	
Apply is focused on the verb in the reinforcement objective	
An average of twenty messages per objective	
Total Score:	

If your total score is:

Less than 11 points: Needs improvement

11 to 16 points: Needs attention

17 to 24 points: Good to go

How well did you score? Did you win a gold medal, or do you need to improve on this principle for the foundation?

Remember the formula $BC = F \times E$. Look at your score, and determine the first small improvements you can make.

If you scored in the "Needs attention" category, you win the bronze medal. It is OK, but you are not there yet. Don't think that winning a bronze medal is almost the same as winning a gold medal. As my coach explained to me, "You did not win the bronze medal, you lost your gold."

If your score falls in the "Needs improvement" range, you did not win a medal. Your reinforcement program is headed in the right direction, but it's not good enough to create great results. Stay critical and remember what Kees told me: "To become a champion, you have to complete the smallest details extremely well."

PRINCIPLE 2. ASSESSMENT

How well did you design the foundation of your reinforcement program? Read each statement below and give yourself points based on the following scale:

Poor: 1 point

Fair: 2 points

Good: 3 points

Excellent: 4 points

Principle 2: Close the 5 Reinforcement Gaps

The knowledge gap can be closed.	
There are opportunities for additional learning (adaptive learning, combination with micro learning).	
The skills gap can be closed.	
Scenarios are used to help the learners identify skills gaps.	
We know what motivates learners and how to avoid demotivation.	
We spend enough time on environment (practicing and asking for feedback).	
The reinforcement program creates enough time to practice.	
It is clear how the new behavior fits into the organization.	
Total Score:	

If your total score is:

Less than 14 points: Needs improvement

14 to 23 points: Needs attention

24 to 32 points: Good to go

How well did you score on this principle? Did you build a foundation that focuses on strengthening the current situation or a foundation that is headed toward a change in behavior?

Check whether you scored a Poor or Fair on one of the eight checkpoints in your assessment. Avoid Poor scores; those will not drive the change. One level up makes a huge difference. If you're critical now, you will be happy during the final analysis of the behavior change.

As Kees often says, "It's easy to become a champion, but it's hard to stay a champion for years." The same goes for behavior change. "It's easy to start the change, but guiding the change to maximum results is harder." Make sure your foundation facilitates the start of the behavior change and the continuation of it.

PRINCIPLE 3. ASSESSMENT

For this last principle of the reinforcement program foundation, check how you performed when designing your foundation. Read each statement below and give yourself points based on the following scale:

Poor: 1 point

Fair: 2 points

Good: 3 points

Excellent: 4 points

Principle 3: Create Measurable Behavior Change

Clearly defined what progress is needed from learners over what period	
Defined what results must be achieved monthly	
Prioritized the improvements I wanted	
Used a verb in each reinforcement objective for measurement purposes	
Created the behavior change questions	
Based measurements on important conditions needed for the behavior change	
Based 25 percent on checking new knowledge and skills	
Can convert reinforcement data into actionable intelligence	
Able to find current issues and predict future ones	
Will collect the right information about all types of learners	
Used a Likert-type scale	
Total score:	

If your total score is:

Less than 20 points: Needs improvement

20 to 32 points: Needs attention

33 to 44 points: Good to go

How well did you score on this final foundation principle? How well did you complete the What, When, and How for your measurement plan? Look at the statements where you scored your design lower. Don't be too easy on yourself. A critical assessment is required for success. As they say, "Garbage in, garbage out."

PRINCIPLE 4. ASSESSMENT

Continue assessing your implementation of the three principles that drive engagement. How did you perform in designing your reinforcement program? Read each statement below and give yourself points based on the following scale:

Poor: 1 point

Fair: 2 points

Good: 3 points

Excellent: 4 points

Principle 4. Provide the Perfect Push and Pull

Achieved perfect balance between push and pull communication	
Continually pushed learners' brains to work and avoided using shortcuts	
Accessed memories from the training event during reinforcement	
Used different methods to pull information (to do, evaluate, and answer questions)	
Stimulated the brain until it reached a baseline level of fluency (easy thoughts)	
Used memory techniques to update knowledge and avoid mistakes	
Total Score:	

If your total score is:

Less than 12 points: Needs improvement

12 to 19 points: Needs attention

20 to 24 points: Good to go

How did you score on this principle? You will see a lot of improvement in your learners if you avoid retraining and focus on application and evaluation. Remember that each phase of the behavior change has its own approach. In the Knowledge and Skills phase, it's an art to test knowledge while at the same time supporting the learners.

PRINCIPLE 5. ASSESSMENT

Consider how you have used Principle 5, "Create Friction and Direction," to keep your learners' brains active. Have you challenged the learners to think about what's new, how they solve this challenge, or how the new information fits with what they already know? Read each statement below and give yourself points based on the following scale:

Poor: 1 point

Fair: 2 points

Good: 3 points

Excellent: 4 points

Principle 5: Create Friction and Direction

The reinforcement program is not predictable.	
Perfect balance exists between friction and direction.	
Just enough direction is provided so the learners avoid getting lost in the content.	
The series of messages uses different patterns.	
The reinforcement program is written in the second person.	
The messages keep their brains alert.	
Social friction is stimulated.	
Communication messages are balanced between specific and general.	
Total Score:	

If your total score is:

Less than 17 points: Needs improvement

17 to 26 points: Needs attention

27 to 32 points: Good to go

If your program needs improvement or requires attention, review the nine actions that create direction and then review the nine actions that create friction. Consider how you can work more of these into your reinforcement program.

PRINCIPLE 6. ASSESSMENT

How did you create the reinforcement flow to balance your learners' skills with the challenges you gave them? How do you motivate the learners to leave their comfort zones? Read each statement below and give yourself points based on the following scale:

Poor: 1 point

Fair: 2 points

Good: 3 points

Excellent: 4 points

Principle 6: Follow the Reinforcement Flow

The program offers perfect flow, balanced between challenges and skills.	
More difficult questions (not answers) are used over time.	
Details in the answers distinguish between correct and incorrect responses.	
Some challenges are out of the learners' comfort zones.	
Skills will develop over time, so the challenges in the scenarios do also.	
The learners feel rewarded by meeting each challenge.	
The CCAF Model is followed.	
A variety of feedback mechanisms keeps learners informed.	
The program moves back and forth between challenging and rewarding learners.	
Learners can see the next goal in order to progress.	
Learners can "rest" or have time to work on their skills.	
Total Score:	

If your total score is:

Less than 22 points: Needs improvement

22 to 35 points: Needs attention

36 to 44 points: Good to go

(continued)

> (*continued*)
>
> If your program needs improvement or attention, check how you organized the feedback and how that helps learners to move into the flow zone. Double-check the flow assessment and see whether your challenges are too difficult or too easy. Are they becoming more difficult over time?

REINFORCEMENT ASSESSMENTS

How strong is your reinforcement program? In other words, how well did you use The 7 Principles of Reinforcement to create results and drive participation? You can check how strong your fundament and engagement of your reinforcement program are. After you have completed two assessments, the fundament assessment and the engagement assessment, you will be able to find your reinforcement lever and know exactly how well you will create results and participation.

Each principle has a principle assessment. If you combine the scores from the principle assessments, you can figure out how strong your foundation is. During my Judo career, we assessed my strength, my weight, and my condition. If one of them under-performed, we adjusted the training program or my diet. Sometimes I had to spend more time on my strength and do extra workouts. But in the end, it's not each individual aspect but the total package that has to be in balance to build a solid foundation to perform and achieve results.

FOUNDATION ASSESSMENT

To calculate your overall score for the foundation, add the total scores for each of the Principles 1, 2, and 3.

My overall score on the Foundation Assessment is: _____

If your total score is:

Less than 45 points: Needs improvement

45 to 71 points: Needs attention

72 to 100 points: Good to go

ENGAGEMENT ASSESSMENT

To calculate your overall score for engagement, add the total scores for each of the Principles 4, 5, and 6.

My overall score on the Engagement Assessment is: _____

If your total score is:

Less than 51 points: Needs improvement

52 to 80 points: Needs attention

81 to 100 points: Good to go

REINFORCEMENT LEVER SCORE FORM

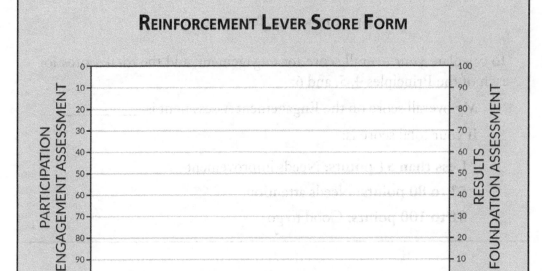

Figure A.1. Blank Reinforcement Lever to Assess Your Own Reinforcement Program

Principle Scores Overview

Principle	Max Score	My Score	Attention	Improvement
1. Master the 3 Phases	24		11–16	< 11
2. Close the 5 Reinforcement Gaps	32		14–23	< 14
3. Create Measurable Behavior Change	44		20–32	< 20
4. Provide the Perfect Push and Pull	24		12–19	< 12
5. Create Friction and Direction	32		17–26	< 17
6. Follow the Reinforcement Flow	44		22–35	< 22

S.A.F.E. Model Assessment

As a reinforcement specialist, your reinforcement messages are like my coach's instructions were during the short breaks in my Judo fights. He didn't have a lot of time to give me instructions. He could give me only useful information, offer one tip at the time, activate learning created during our training sessions, inspire me, and address me in the second person. He used the S.A.F.E. model to the max.

How well are you using the S.A.F.E. model to craft your messages? Use the assessment below to find improvements you could make. Check your reinforcement messages. If you meet the criteria, give yourself 1 point for yes and 0 points for no in the Y/N column.

Then multiply the number in the Y/N column by the number in the Weight column and sum the numbers. The total score indicates your use of the S.A.F.E. model.

Criteria	Y/N	Weight	Y/N × Weight
Is the message written in the second person?		3	
Is all excess text skipped?		2	
Is your bulleted list active case?		3	
Did you avoid words like "remember"?		1	
Did you avoid words like "it's important"?		1	
Does every assignment have a time element?		3	
Does the medium you use activate the learners' memories?		2	
Does each item contain only one question?		3	
Is the introduction to the question specific?		2	
Did you avoid using the words "you must"?		1	
Is the question specific?		2	
Is the average length of the message under four hundred characters?		2	

Is the text inspiring to the learner?		2	
Is the maximum length of a sentence seventeen words?		2	
Does the title of your message reflect the essence of its content?		1	
Total score			

Check your score. If your total score is:

Less than 13 points: we advise a *no go* and rewrite

14 to 19 points: needs improvement

20 to 24 points: needs attention

25 to 30 points: ready to go

To analyze more in detail and determine which element of the S.A.F.E model you can improve on, use the following list to see what criteria reflects what S.A.F.E. model element.

Criteria	S.A.F.E Model
Is the message written in the second person?	Style
Is all excess text skipped?	Focus
Is your bulleted list active case?	Active
Did you avoid words like "remember"?	Style
Did you avoid words like "it's important"?	Style
Does every assignment have a time element?	Active
Does the medium you use activate the learners' memories?	Active
Does each item contain only one question?	Focus
Is the introduction to the question specific?	Focus
Did you avoid using the words "you must"?	Style
Is the question specific?	Focus
Is the average length of the message under four hundred characters?	Easy to Read
Is the text inspiring to the learner?	Easy to Read
Is the maximum length of a sentence seventeen words?	Easy to Read
Does the title of your message reflect the essence of its content?	Focus

RESOURCES

Abramovich, S., Schunn, C., & Higashi, R.M. (2013). Are badges useful in education? It depends upon the type of badge and expertise of learner. *Educational Technology Research and Development, 61*, 217–232.

Ajzen, I., (1988). Theory of Planned Behavior. 179–211.

Anderson, J.R. (1994). *Learning and Memory: An Integrated Approach.* Hoboken, NJ: John Wiley & Sons. http://tocs.ulb.tu-darmstadt.de/89959310.pdf.

Andrews, S., & Feinberg, S. (1999). Developing and implementing effective web-based surveys. *STC's 46th Annual Conference Proceedings,* Cincinnati, Ohio, 1999. http://www.stc-va.org/proceedings/ConfProceed/1999/PDFs/046.pdf.

Aoki, K., & Elasmar, M. (2000). Opportunities and challenges of a web survey: A field experiment. Paper presented at the 55th Annual Conference of the American Association for Public Opinion Research. Portland, Oregon, 2000.

ATD. (2014). State of the industry report. http://files.astd.org/Research/Infographics/SOIR-2014-Infographic.pdf?_ga=1.228043741.1320061770.1449678068.

Bailey, K.D. (1987). *Methods of Social Research.* London: Free Press.

Barata, G., Gama, S., Jorge, J., & Gonçalves, D. (2013). Improving participation and learning with gamification. Paper presented at Gamification '13. Stratford, Ontario, Canada, 2013.

Bauman, S., Jobity, N., Airey, J., & Atak, H. (2000). Invites, intros and incentives: Lessons from a web survey. Paper presented at the 55th Annual Conference of the American Association for Public Opinion Research. Portland, Oregon, 2000.

Beck, L., & Ajzen, I. (1991). Predicting dishonest actions using the theory of planned behavior. *Journal of Research and Personality, 25,* 285–301.

Bersin, J. Meet the Modern Learner. http://www.slideshare.net/heytodd/the-modern-learner-infographic-final-v4120414.

Bjork, E.L. (2011). How we learn versus how we think we learn: Desirable difficulties in theory and practice, introduction to desirable difficulties, spacing, generation, interleaving, perceptual desirable difficulties, interactions between desirable difficulties. http://bjorklab.psych.ucla.edu/research.html#itemII.

Bjork, E.L. (2011). Learning categories and concepts (inductive learning). http://bjorklab.psych.ucla.edu/research.html#itemIII.

Bjork, E.L. (2011). Goal-directed forgetting, retrieval-induced forgetting, directed forgetting. http://bjorklab.psych.ucla.edu/research.html#itemIV.

Bjork, R.A. (1975). Retrieval as a memory modifier: An interpretation of negative recency and related phenomena. In R.L. Solso (Ed.), *Information Processing and Cognition: The Loyola Symposium*. Mahwah, NJ: Lawrence Erlbaum.

Blake, Jenny. National Institute of General Medical Sciences, "Circadian Rhythms Fact Sheet," last modified October 1, 2015.

Bosnjak, M. (2001). Participation in non-restricted web surveys. A typology and explanatory model for item-nonresponse. In U.-D. Reips & M. Bosnjak (Eds.), *Dimensions of Internet Science*. Lengerich, Germany: Pabst Science Publishers, 193–208.

Bowker, D. (1999). Constructing the client-computer interface: Guidelines for design and implementation of web-based surveys. Summary Report 99–15, Social and Economic Sciences Research Center, Washington State University, Pullman, Washington.

Brennan, M., Rae, N., & Parackal, M. (1999). Survey-based experimental research via the web: Some observations. *Marketing Bulletin, 10*, 83–92. http://marketing-bulletin.massey.ac.nz/article10/article9.asp.

Brinkerhoff, Robert O. The 40/20/40 Model. http://www.leadershippipelineinstitute.com/impact-high-impact-learning-402040model.aspx.

Brown, Peter C., Roediger III, Henry L., & McDaniel, Mark A. (2014). Make it stick: The science of successful learning. *Learning Solutions*. http://www.learningsolutionsmag.com/articles/1354/brain-science-the-neuroscience-of-teaching-and-learning.

Bunchball, Inc. (2010). Gamification 101: An introduction to the use of game dynamics to influence behavior. Retrieved from http://www.bunchball.com/sites/default/files/downloads/gamification101.pdf.

Burns, Ralph. Information impact and factors affecting recall. ERIC Clearinghouse. http://eric.ed.gov/?id=ED258639.

Chun, M.M., Golumb, J.D., & Turk-Browne, N.B. (2011). A taxonomy of external and internal attention. *The Annual Review of Psychology, 62*, 73–101.

Csikszentmihalyi, M. (1990). *Flow: The Psychology of Optimal Experience*. New York: Harper & Row, pp. 195–206 of *Oxford Library of Psychology*. https://books.google.nl/books?hl=nl&lr=&id=6IyqCNBD6oIC&oi=fnd&pg=PA195&dq=flow+theory+csikszentmihalyi&ots=ILI9MF0hyC&sig=oXi-f4A6D0ZCm1nSlveUpkKkiRQ#v=onepage&q=flow%20theory%20csikszentmihalyi&f=false.

Csikszentmihalyi, M. (1978). Intrinsic rewards and emergent motivation. In M.R. Lepper & D. Greene (Eds.), *The Hidden Costs of Reward: New Perspectives on the Psychology of Human Motivation*. Mahwah, NJ: Lawrence Erlbaum, 205–216.

Colgrass, N. (May 14, 2015). Our attention span now worse than goldfish's. *USA Today*.

Comley, P. (1998). Guide to web site evaluation. *MRS Research*, June 1998. http://www.virtualsurveys.com/papers/webeval.html.

Couper, M.P. (2000). Web surveys: A review of issues and approaches. *Public Opinion Quarterly, 64*, 464–494.

Couper, M.P. (2001). Web surveys: The questionnaire design challenge. *EProceedings of the ISI 2001*. The 53rd Session of the ISI, Seoul, Korea, August 22–29, 2001. http://134.75.100.178/isi2001/.

Couper, M.P., Traugott, M., & Lamias, M. (2001). Web survey design and administration. *Public Opinion Quarterly, 65*, 230–253.

Deci, E.L., & Ryan, R.M. (2000). The "what" and "why" of goal pursuits: Human needs and the self-determination of behavior. *Psychological Inquiry, 11*(4), 227–268.

de Jonge, Mario, Tabbers, Huib K., & Rikers, Remy M.J.P. (June 2015). The effect of testing on the retention of coherent and incoherent text material. *Educational Psychology Review, 27*(2), 305–315.

Deterding, S., Dixon, D., Khaled, R., & Nacke, L. (2011). From game design elements to gamefulness: Defining gamification. In *Proceedings of the 15th International Academic MindTrek Conference: Envisioning Future Media Environments*, 9–15.

Dicheva, D., Dichev, C., Agre, G., & Angelova, G. (2015). Gamification in education: A systematic mapping study. *Educational Technology & Society, 18*.

Dillman, D.A., Tortora, R.D., & Bowker, D. (1998). Influence of plain vs. fancy design on response rates for web surveys. *Proceedings of Survey Methods Section*, 1998.

Dohrenwend, B.S. (1965). Some effects of open and closed questions on respondents' awareness. *Human Organization, 24*, 175–184.

Domínguez, A., Saenz-de-Navarrete, J., De-Marcos, L., Fernández-Sanz, L., Pagés, C., & Martínez-Herráiz, J.-J. (2013). Gamifying learning experiences: Practical implications and outcomes. *Computers & Education, 63*, 380–392.

Dweck, Carol S. (2007). *Mindset: The New Psychology of Success*. New York: Ballantine Books.

Eagen, T. (2016). The eight-second attention span. *The New York Times*, January 22.

Educause. (2011). 7 Things you should know about gamification. Retrieved from http://www.educause.edu/library/resources/7-things-you-should-know-about-gamification.

Falkner, N.J., & Falkner, K.E. (2014). Whither, badges? or wither, badges!: A metastudy of badges in computer science education to clarify effects, significance and influence. In *Proceedings of the 14th Koli Calling International Conference on Computing Education Research*, 127–135.

Festinger, L. (1954). A theory of social comparison processes. *Human Relations, 7*(2), 117–140.

Foddy, W. (1993). *Constructing Questions for Interviews and Questionnaires: Theory and Practice in Social Research*. Cambridge: Cambridge University Press.

Gagné, R. (1985). *The Conditions of Learning and the Theory of Instruction* (4th ed.). New York: Holt, Rinehart, and Winston.

Gal, E., & Nachmias, R. (2011). On-line learning and performance support using performance support platforms. *Performance Improvement Journal, 50*(8), 25–32.

Gatch, C.L., & Kendzierski, D. (1990). Predicting exercise intentions: The theory of planned behavior. *Research Quarterly for Exercise and Sport, 61*(1), 100–102.

Gausby, A. (2015). Attention spans. Mississauga, Ontario: Microsoft Canada.

Godin, G., Valois, P., Lepage, L., & Desharnais, R. (1992). Predictors of smoking behavior: An application of Ajzen's theory of planned behavior. *British Journal of Addition, 87*, 1335–1343.

Gonier, D.E. (1999). The emperor gets new clothes. In Towards Validation. Online Research Day. An ARF Emerging Issue Workshop. New York: Advertising Research Foundation, 8–13. http://www.dmsdallas.com/emporere/emporer.html.

Gräf, L. (2002). Assessing internet questionnaires: The online pretest lab. In B. Batinic, U.-D. Reips, M. Bosnjak, and A. Werner (Eds.), *Online Social Sciences.* Seattle, WA: Hogrefe & Huber, 73–93.

Gyorki, D.E., Shaw, T., Nicholson, J., Baker, C., Pitcher, M., Skandarajah, A., & Segelov, E. (June 2013). Improving the impact of didactic resident training with online spaced education. Mann GB. *ANZ Journal of Surgery, 83*(6),477–480. http://www.ncbi.nlm.nih.gov/pubmed/23617607.

Hamari, J., Koivisto, J., & Sarsa, H. (2014). Does gamification work? A literature review of empirical studies on gamification. In *Proceedings of the 47th Hawaii International Conference on System Science* (HICSS), Waikoloa, Hawaii, 3025–3034.

Ibanez, M. ., Di-Serio, A., & Delgado-Kloos, C. (2014). Gamification for engaging computer science students in learning activities: A case study. *Transactions on Learning Technologies*, (3), 1–1.

Internet Rogator. (1998). Internet Rogator help with surveying. http://www.internet-rogator.com/htm/help.htm.

Jones, B.A., Madden, G.J., Wengreen, H.J., Aguilar, S.S., & Desjardins, E.A. (2014). Gamification of dietary decision-making in an elementary-school cafeteria. *PLOS ONE, 9*(4), e93872.

Kapp, K.M. (2012). *The Gamification of Learning and Instruction: Game-Based Methods and Strategies for Training and Education.* Hoboken, NJ: John Wiley & Sons.

Machado, M., & Tao, E. (2007). Blackboard vs. Moodle: Comparing user experience of learning management systems. In *Proceedings of Frontiers in Education Conference-Global Engineering: Knowledge Without Borders, Opportunities Without Passports*, S4J-7. FIE'07. 37th Annual Conference, Milwaukee, Wisconsin.

Kahneman, Daniel. (2011). *Thinking Fast and Slow.* New York: Farrar, Straus and Giroux.

Karpicke1, Jeffrey D., & Roediger III, Henry L. (2008). The critical importance of retrieval for learning. *Science, 319*(5865), 966–968. http://science.sciencemag.org/content/319/5865/966.

Kashima, Y., Gallois, C. & McCamish, M. (1993). Theory of reasoned action and cooperative behavior: It takes two to use a condom. *British Journal of Social Psychology, 32*, 227–239.

Kohn, A. (2014). Brain science: The neuroscience of teaching and learning. *Learning Solutions Magazine*. http://www.learningsolutionsmag.com/articles/1354/brain-science-the-neuroscience-of-teaching-and-learning.

Kimiecik, J. (1992). Predicting vigorous physical activity of corporate employees: Comparing the theories of reasoned action and planned behavior. *Journal of Sport and Exercise Psychology, 14*, 192–206.

Kirkpatrick, D. (1994). The four-level training evaluation model. *Evaluating Training Programs*. San Francisco: Berrett-Koehler.

Knapp, F., & Heidingsfelder, M. (2001). Drop-out analysis: Effects of the survey design. In U.-D. Reips & M. Bosnjak (Eds.), *Dimensions of Internet Science*. Lenerich, Germany: Pabst Science Publishers, 221–230.

Kwak, N., & Radler, B.T. (1999). A comparison between mail and web-based surveys: Response pattern, data quality, and characteristics of respondents. Paper presented at 1999 Annual Research Conference, organized by Midwest Association for Public Opinion Research, Chicago, November 1999.

Lazarsfeld, P.F. (1944). The controversy over detailed interviews—An offer for negotiation. *Public Opinion Quarterly, 8*, 38–60.

Lozar Manfreda, K. (2001). Web survey errors. Doctoral dissertation. Ljubljana, Slovenia: Faculty of Social Sciences, University of Ljubljana.

Lozar Manfreda, K., Batagelj, Z., & Vehovar, V. (2002). Design of web survey questionnaires: Three basic experiments. *Journal of Computer Mediated Communication, 7*. http://www.ascusc.org/jcmc/vol7/issue3/vehovar.htmlOpen-ended vs.Close-endedQuestions inWebQuestionnaires177.

McDermott, Kathleen B., & Roediger III, Henry L. (2014), Memory (encoding, storage, retrieval) St. Louis, MO: Washington University. http://nobaproject.com/modules/memory-encoding-storage-retrieval.

McSpadden, K. (May 14, 2015). You now have a shorter attention span than a goldfish. *Time* magazine.

Medina, J. (2008). *Brain Rules: 12 Principles for Surviving and Thriving at Work, Home, and School*, Seattle, WA: Pear Press.

Mehta, R., & Sivadas, E. (1995). Comparing response rates and response content in mail versus electronic mail surveys. *Journal of the Market Research Society, 37*, 429–439.

Minter, R.M. (2013). Teaching the teacher–Spaced education as a novel approach to teaching interns to teach. Commentary. *American Journal of Surgery, 206*(1), 128–129. http://www.ncbi.nlm.nih.gov/pubmed/23790216.

Moreno, Roxana, & Mayer, Richard E. (2004). Personalized messages that promote science learning in virtual environments. *Journal of Educational Psychology, 96*(1), 165–173. http://psycnet.apa.org/index.cfm?fa=buy.optionToBuy&id=2004–11358–014.

Mosher, B., & Gottfredson, C. (2011). *Innovative Performance Support: Strategies and Practices for Learning in the Workflow*. New York: McGraw-Hill.

Nichols, E., & Sedivi, B. (1998). Economic data collection via the web: A census bureau case study. *Proceedings of the Section on Survey Research Methods.* American Statistical Association, Alexandria, Virginia, 366–371. http://surveys.over.net/method/papers/proc98.wpd.

Nicholson, S. (2012). A user-centered theoretical framework for meaningful gamification. *Games+ Learning+ Society, 8,* 1.

Parker, D., Manstead, A.S.R., Stradling, S.G., & Reason, J.T. (1992). Intention to commit driving violations: An application of the theory of planned behavior. *Journal of Applied Psychology, 77*(1), 94–101.

Pashler, H. (1998). *The Psychology of Attention.* Cambridge, MA, MIT Press.

Payne, S.L. (1980). *The Art of Asking Questions.* Princeton NJ: Princeton University Press.

Pilieci, V. (May 12, 2015). Canadians now have shorter attention span than goldfish thanks to portable devices: Microsoft study. *National Post.*

PolicyViz. (January 29, 2016). The attention span statistic fallacy.

Radvansky, Gabriel A. (2010). *Human Memory* (2nd ed.). New York: Routledge, 46.

Reips, U.-D. (2000). The web experiment method: Advantages, disadvantages, and solutions. In M.H. Birnbaum (Ed.), *Psychological Experiments on the Internet.* San Diego, CA: Academic Press.

Robinson, L. (1998). Behavior change model, by Les Robinson of Social Change Media in Australia. Think Differently, Written on May 7, 2007 by Dr. Lauchlan A. K. Mackinnon.

Roediger III, Henry L., & Karpicke, Jeffrey D. (2006). Test-enhanced learning: Taking memory tests improves long-term retention. *Psychological Science, 17*(3), 249. http://pss.sagepub.com/content/17/3/249.short.

Salen, K., & Zimmerman, E. (2004). *Rules of Play: Game Design Fundamentals.* Cambridge, MA: MIT Press.

Sarma, Sanjay, & Zolot, Ken. (2016). MIT and learning: Integrated digital and open source learning. Presentation at Masie Learning Conference, Orlando, Florida.

Schaefer, D.R., & Dillman, D.A. (1998). Development of a standard e-mail methodology: Results of an experiment. *Public Opinion Quarterly, 62,* 378–397. http://survey.sesrc.wsu.edu/dillman/papers/E-Mailppr.pdf.

Schuman, H., Ludwig, J., & Krosnick, J.A. (1986). The perceived threat of nuclear war, salience, and open questions. *Public Opinion Quarterly, 50,* 519–536.

Schuman, H., & Presser, S. (1979). The open and closed question. *American Sociological Review, 44,* 692–712.

Schuman, H., & Presser, S. (1996). *Questions and Answers in Attitude Surveys.* New York: Academic Press.

Schuman, H., & Scott, J. (1987). Problems in the use of survey questions to measure public opinion. *Science, 236,* 957–959.

Shank, P. (October 27, 2016). What do you know: Should we train "digital natives" differently? ATD Science of Learning Blog.

Sheatsley, P.B. (1983). Questionnaire construction and item writing. In P.H. Rossi, J.D. Wright, & A.B. Anderson (Eds.), *Handbook of Survey Research*. New York: Academic Press, 195–230.

Silverman, Rachel Emma. (2012, October 26). So much training, so little to show for it. Wall Street Journal.com. http://www.wsj.com/articles/SB1000142405297020442590457807295051855 8328.

Skinner, B.F. (1988). *About Behaviorism*. New York: Random House.

Skinner, E., Furrer, C., Marchand, G., & Kindermann, T. (2008). Engagement and disaffection in the classroom: Part of a larger motivational dynamic? *Journal of Educational Psychology, 100*, 765–781

Sohlberg, M.M., & Mateer, C.A. (2001). Improving attention and managing attentional problems: Adapting rehabilitation techniques to adults with ADD. *Annals of the New York Academy of Sciences, 931*, 359–375.

Snyder, C.R., & Lopez, Shane J. (2011). *Oxford Handbook of Positive Psychology* (2nd ed.). Oxford: Oxford University Press.

Storm, Benjamin C., Bjork, Robert A., & Storm, Jennifer C. (2010). Optimizing retrieval as a learning event: When and why expanding retrieval practice enhances long-term retention. *Memory & Cognition, 38*(2), 244–253.

Sturgeon, K., & Winter, S. (1999). International marketing on the world wide web. New opportunities for research: What works, what does not and what is next. *Proceedings of the ESOMAR Worldwide Internet Conference Net Effects*. London, February 1999, 191–200.

Sudman, S., & Bradburn, N. (1974). *Response Effects in Surveys: A Review and Synthesis*. Chicago: Aldine.

Sudman, S., & Bradburn, N. (1991). The current status of questionnaire research. In P.P. Biemer, R.M. Groves, L.E. Lyberg, N.A. Mathiowetz, & S. Sudman (Eds.), *Measurement Errors in Surveys*. Hoboken, NJ: John Wiley & Sons.

Sweller J. (1994). Cognitive load theory, learning difficulty, and instructional design. *Learning and Instruction*, pp. 295–312.

Thaler, Richard H. (2015). *Misbehaving: The Making of Behavioral Economics*. New York: W. W. Norton & Company.

Thaler, Richard H. (2015). Hidden brain podcasts by NPR–Interview.

Thaler, Richard H., & Sunstein, Cass R. (2008). *Nudge: Improving Decisions About Health, Wealth and Happiness*. New Haven, CT: Yale University Press.

Thalheimer, Will. How much do people forget? http://willthalheimer.typepad.com/files/how-much-do-people-forget- v12–14–2010.pdf.

TED Talks. Our brains: Predictably irrational. https://www.ted.com/playlists/74/our_brains_predictablyirrational.

The testing effect: Retrieval-induced forgetting. http://bjorklab.psych.ucla.edu/research.html#itemI.

Weinberg, Robert, & Gould, Daniel. (2014). Three types of intrinsic motivation. *Foundations of Sport and Exercise Psychology* (6th ed.). Champaign, IL: Human Kinetics.

Weinreich, H., Obendorf, H., Herder, E., &, Mayer, M. (February 2008). Not quite the average: An empirical study of web use. *ACM Transactions on the Web, 2*(1).

Willke, J., Adams, C.O., & Girnius, Z. (1999). Internet testing: A landmark study of the differences between mall intercept and on-line interviewing in the United States. *Proceedings of the ESOMAR Worldwide Internet Conference Net Effects.* London, February 21–23, pp. 145–157.

Wilson, Karen, & Korn, James H. (2007). Attention during lectures: Beyond ten minutes. *Teaching of Psychology, 34*(2), 85–89.

Zichermann, G., & Cunningham, C. (2011). *Gamification by Design: Implementing Game Mechanics in Web and Mobile Apps.* Sebastopol, CA: O'Reilly Media, Inc.

ABOUT THE AUTHORS

ANTHONIE WURTH, FOUNDER OF MINDMARKER

Anthonie Wurth founded Mindmarker, a world leader in reinforcement training, in Holland in 2006. In addition to being a learning and reinforcement expert, Anthonie is a former Olympic athlete in Judo. He represented the Dutch Judo team for more than 10 years and was European champion in 1991.

After competing in the Barcelona Olympics in 1992, he started a career with a large European training company. During his time there, he found that the lack of reinforcement held learners back from achieving results. To solve this problem for organizations around the world, Anthonie used his Olympic background and extensive training experience to build his unique methodology, "The 7 Principles of Reinforcement."

Anthonie grew up in a family where lasting results were top of mind. His brother, Kees, was also an international Judo champion and represented the Dutch Judo team for many years. Their grandfather and parents owned successful companies in Holland. In 1993, Anthonie married the daughter of his Judo coach. He enjoyed all the conversations about peak performance and lasting results.

His first book, *Locked in Shanghai*, is about the freedom of thinking needed for performance. Fascinated by the power of the brain and how people apply what they have learned, he created "The 7 Principles of Reinforcement." His writing has been featured in many blog posts and articles.

Anthonie is a frequent presenter at international learning conferences and an expert in training reinforcement science. As Anthonie likes to say, "You don't win medals because you know. You win medals because you apply."

KEES WURTH, CEO OF MINDMARKER

The importance of training was established at a young age for Mindmarker CEO Kees Wurth. As a child, he trained long hours with top Judo instructors in The Netherlands with the goal of becoming a national champion, which he later accomplished.

Kees emigrated to the United States in 1993 to pursue the American dream. He is an entrepreneur who has successfully started and sold a number of companies. His drive to "get better every day" is contagious and creates extraordinary people and teams that collectively create success and happiness.

Kees believes: "Learning never stops. In order to perform at your best, you constantly have to evaluate what you do and use the feedback others provide you."

ABOUT MINDMARKER

Mindmarker is a global leader in training reinforcement. As pioneers in training reinforcement, Anthonie Wurth started the company in Amsterdam, The Netherlands, in 2006. In 2013 they moved their headquarters to Atlanta, Georgia, and maintained offices in Amsterdam hosting IT and sales teams. In 2017 the company supported learners in more than 100 countries, and today continues to be recognized as an authority on training reinforcement.

Mindmarker helps learners transfer learning into application. Together with clients, they create and deliver adaptive reinforcement programs to increase the impact of learning. The outcome is a personalized adaptive learning journey that inspires and guides learners in the transformation of learning into application in their jobs.

HOW WE STARTED

After training for and participating in the Barcelona Olympic Games in 1992, Anthonie Wurth spent 10 years as a corporate trainer. During that time, he identified a gap between training and actual results or behavior change from training. Wanting to solve this gap, Anthonie combined various scientific studies about behavior change with his experiences as an athlete to create an innovative and unique methodology to create lasting behavior change.

HOW WE DO IT

Everybody recognizes the need for reinforcing training. Without reinforcement there is no impact. The biggest question is "How do I build an effective reinforcement program?" Over the last 12 years, Mindmarker has developed an effective method to build reinforcement programs that create long-term behavior change. Combined with award-winning web and mobile technology, the company is able to send the adaptive reinforcement program to individual learners to support them in creating desired behavior change. Learners receive short and carefully planned learning nuggets, based on their specific need, on an app or web browser.

What We Offer

Mindmarker shares its methodology with learning professionals to help them create impact from training. The Mindmarker portal allows learning professionals to build programs and send bite-sized pieces of content and questions to learners globally. Mindmarker has a dedicated team of specialists providing assistance and support to clients when building reinforcement programs. Mindmarker also assists in analyzing the results of the programs to create better training programs and improve business results.

Who Uses Mindmarker?

We help clients around the world and create impact in every industry and for every type of training. Sales, leadership, product, on-boarding, and compliance training all benefit from using a Mindmarker reinforcement program. Whether in the financial, retail, pharmaceutical, or any other industry, every learner and every business can benefit from the behavior change Mindmarker brings. With focus on the individual learner, we gain their trust and support to help them become better at their jobs.

Why We Do It

We do this because we are passionate about helping people get better at their jobs. For many years, learners did not receive the support and tools to actually change and improve. We now have a methodology and the technology to help learners get better, advance their careers, and help their companies perform better.

INDEX